BRING YOUR BEST GAME

From Sharpshooter

To Global Businessman

To Artist

By
John Kirk

J Kirk Publishing
2024

"If you really want to do something, you'll find a way. If you don't, you'll find an excuse."
— Jim Rohn

"Successful people keep moving. They make mistakes, but they don't quit."
— Conrad Hilton

"If you can dream it, you can do it."
— Walt Disney

CONTENTS

I

SHAPING MY VIEW OF THE WORLD

CHAPTER 1

A CHILD IN EUROPE

I was seven, and an Army brat, standing with my mother on a tarmac in Nashville, Tennessee, boarding a plane for a flight to New York City and then on to Paris, France. At the time, I had no idea of the adventure I was embarking on that May morning in 1955 and that my life would change, and change again, in directions that I couldn't yet imagine.

In May the temperature was mild during the days, but it was cool that early misty morning when Mom and I climb the planes stairs. I could smell aviation fuel as the breeze changed direction. Years later I would look upon that scene and be reminded of the final airport scene in the movie Casablanca, minus the fog. As I settled in my seat, my stomach was churning with the excitement of this new adventure, but I didn't know that this journey would be the beginning of a lifetime of adventures. Traveling and working in forty-two countries and living in three. Meeting global icons—Sean Connery, Louis Armstrong, Colin Powell, and Diana Ross to name a few. Experiencing tragedies— being in New York Times Square on 911 when the planes hit, seeing the poverty in Mumbai, losing family and friends. But during it all, I inhaled the wonders of the world—the allure of Paris in the springtime, Picasso's masterpieces, and the captivating photography of Henri Cartier-Bresson.

Reassignments are a part of military life, but it always comes as a shock when the orders are given. Given they were, everyone, two, or if you were lucky three years. Which explains why I went to thirteen schools during my twelve years until graduating from high school. That sounds difficult but it had its advantages. Seeing places and experiencing things that many people would never have the chance to do. It also forced me to learn the art of adapting. Each move meant new people and places with little time to assimilate. But even with the challenges it gave me the beginning of an extraordinary rich life.

With this move, Mom and I weren't scheduled to join my dad in Metz, France for six weeks, but we were left with the task of packing and shipping our household, selling our car and moving out of base housing. Mom was heroic, going through the To Do list and getting it all done. It did require her tenacity and forcefulness to cut through the military bureaucracy or we wouldn't have made the deadlines of clearing post and getting to France.

After those tasks were completed, we took the last two weeks before departing for France to visit family in Kentucky, West Virginia, and Tennessee. Our last stop was to see my aunt, uncle and cousin in McMinnville, Tennessee. While there, I visited a rural school where my uncle's mother was a teacher. I didn't know why I was asked to visit the school; I thought it was to get out of everyone's hair, but it turned out that the students wanted to hear my story of moving so much and talk to someone setting off on an adventure in another part of the world.

At the end of the dirt road from the school to the main highway, my aunt and uncle owned a local grocery store and diner. My reward for attending school was going to their store to get a hamburger, fries, and a soft drink. I took notice of the attention my aunt gave to crafting each hamburger. The beef patty was thin on the edges and just thick enough in the middle, which allowed for more uniform cooking and some crispness around the edges. The patty was a third or more fat, finely ground, and sourced locally. It was cooked on a flat-top grill which was also used to cook bacon, eggs, and other foods. The transfer of those flavors to my hamburger was extraordinary. The bun was a plain white hamburger bun which complemented the meat, and no other ingredients like sesame seeds were on it. My aunt added mustard, mayonnaise, lettuce, tomato, onion, and pickles. It was so juicy I needed a lot of napkins when eating it and today I would love to find a burger that good again. The experience was a true example of doing things the right way.

Our six weeks were up, our family visits completed, and it was time to continue our journey, to New York and then Paris.

Upon landing in New York City, after a two-and-a-half-hour flight, we found the military arrivals desk and cued up for transportation to our hotel. Our luggage was checked in at the bus and kept by the military to be loaded on the plane. We only had carry-on bags such as Mom's makeup case.

The hotel was a no frills one with a plain lobby, furniture, and few decorations, more like a doctor's waiting room. Our room was basic as well: it had two twin beds with a side table between them, one dresser with mirror, one side chair, and a couple of photos on the wall that had faded with time. After all, it was contracted by the U.S. military and no frills were expected. We were told that we were on a Military Air Transport Service (MATS) flight to Paris that evening, but that was subject to change, and we would be updated during the day. We ate lunch in the hotel, I, of course, had a burger and fries. We waited in our room until later in the afternoon when word came for us to catch the military bus to New York's Idlewild Airport. That meant we would wait at the airport for a few hours before boarding. The practice of the military is to—hurry up and wait, which we did in the airport boarding area.

Finally, we heard the pre-boarding announcement and got in line to board. Once boarding started, we were asked again to show our passports and tickets. We boarded, found our seats, and settled in for our thirteen-hour flight from New York to Paris. That included two stops along the way for refueling: Gander, Newfoundland and Shannon, Ireland. Those two stops were stressful because we had to wait at each stop for the refueling operations to be completed. Each stop only increased my frustration, as I wanted to get to our destination.

The one positive thing was that we flew on the latest and greatest plane, at that time, a Trans World Airways (TWA) Super Constellation. Nicknamed the "Super Connie." The plane was sleek and stylish, with a triple-tail design and dolphin-shaped fuselage.

A few years ago, I saw one at Frankfurt airport on display with Lufthansa Airlines colors and markings. It was smaller than I remembered but it's still a cool looking plane.

The flight wasn't a great one. The turbo-propeller plane went up, down, and sideways, as winds and weather pushed it around. This movement didn't go well with my already churning stomach and you can guess the results. I hadn't used the toilet for a couple of days, while eating food regularly. The hectic schedule, being anxious, and the excitement of the trip caused bowel problems. During the flight one of the three restrooms on the plane was dedicated just for me, which didn't make me popular with my fellow travelers. Mom was also not doing well on the flight either. She didn't like to fly and had taken sleeping pills to help, but she was still wide awake and tense. I asked her how many pills she took, "I only took a few" she said. But I remember her taking a couple and at least one more on the plane and I became concerned that she would be harmed in some way by taking too many pills. As it turned out her anxiety, metabolism, or something counteracted them, and she wasn't harmed. This flight experience stayed with me for many years, making me anxious about flying. It wasn't until the 1980's when I had to fly almost daily for business that I acclimated to the world of flight. The act of living on a plane during the week settled my anxiety.

I remember our TWA pilot coming on the intercom to announce that we had "Just passed the point of no return." Apparently, it was the thing to announce in those days, but being an uneducated flyer, this sounded scary to me. What it really meant was that if there was a problem, we would have to continue forward since we no longer had enough fuel to turn back. If in trouble and the concept of turning back and returning home was a comforting one for me, that comfort had been taken away. I didn't get any sleep on the flight and spent the time, when not in the restroom, thinking about my family's life up to then. After WWII, Dad had gone back to his hometown, Kermit, West Virginia, married my mom, who lived in a neighboring town Warfield, Kentucky and got a job to make a life for them. I came along a little over a year later in July of 1947. After twenty months of working various jobs including as a postal clerk, mom and dad concluded they had two choices to create the life they had envisioned. Dad would either go work in the local coal mines or go back in the Army, Dad reenlisted in the Army.

Our family had already been stationed at four military bases—which included the one we just departed Fort Knox, Kentucky our second time there. I don't remember anything about the first two bases: Fort Knox, the first time, and Fort Belvoir, Virginia. Our third base, Fort Leonard Wood, Missouri and our second time at Fort Knox stood out for both good and bad reasons. We were stationed at Fort Leonard Wood for twenty-two months between 1951 and 1953 and I was four and five during that time. Dad was assigned to this training base because of his WWII experience, his Bronze Star medals, Purple Heart, and having the rank of Sergeant First Class. His assignment was to prepare troops to join the fight in Korea.

There was no base housing, and little civilian housing available, so dad rented the best place he could find. It had a combination living and kitchen area, one bedroom, and a small bath. The construction was of a wood frame, standard sheet rock on the inside, some insulation and a waterproof tar/paper mixture that was a sealant to the weather—the structure was commonly called a tar paper shack. My bed was an Army cot with Army sheets and a wool blanket with a black US stamped in the center. I really didn't care about the house or sleeping arrangements because I was with Mom and Dad.

Some of my happiest times there were when I could play outside and watch Dad work on our car or toss the baseball back and forth. In the winter I would bundle up and put on my flop-eared cap to keep warm. Another fun event was when I received a Hopalong Cassidy cowboy outfit for Christmas. The outfit consisted of chaps, vest, hat, and two plastic six shooters, which I was proud to wear. I also loved going to the base for holiday dinners with the troops. The food was delicious, and the servers always gave out large portions. Upon their graduation from training and before deployment, a group of soldiers presented me with a pet rabbit. I loved it except when Mom and Dad later had to give me the unwelcome news that we couldn't keep it, as we had no place for it. Having to give up the gift became more painful when dad later learned that most of those soldiers had been killed in a major battle in Korea. He was devastated and questioned if he had done enough to train them.

Unfortunately, there were other negatives. It seems that our duplex had been built over an exotic snake habitat. The snakes had escaped from a traveling show, long since gone. This habitat was still active, and we would see several of them emerge from under the house and roam the yard in the evening. When the sun came up, they usually retreated under the house. One time I was outside using a porcelain potty while Mom was hanging the laundry on the line when she saw a snake coming out from under the house moving in my direction between her and me. She immediately ran inside and got a bucket of boiling water from the stove. When she returned, the snake had raised up on the forward portion of its body and extended its hood. I was frozen in place as I looked at the approaching snake's dark menacing eyes. Mom ran forward, threw the hot water on it, and the snake immediately retreated under the house. I've hated snakes ever since.

Our duplex was one of three that sat across the road from the landlord's general store. Of course, the prices at that store were much higher than they should've been because he had a captive audience. The road we had to cross was a two-lane highway, which was a major highway in the early '50s, and the cars would go by at fifty to seventy miles per hour. Once Mom, Dad, and I were going to the store and started to cross the highway. "Stop, a car is coming" , Mom said. "Oh, we can make it," Dad replied. I decided to break from them and run across the road. Half-way across I heard the screeching of tires. As I jumped in the ditch on the far side of the road I could hear and feel a car going past me. After swerving and slamming on the brakes, the driver finally got his 3900-pound 1951 Buick Special under control and stopped. He got out of his car and came back to see if I was okay, and to tell Mom and Dad how stupid they were to let me cross the road. Mom and Dad apologized, and I ended up getting a lecture. I know now that I might have died by acting on impulse instead of waiting for my parents to decide. Acting on impulse can be debated, but in this case, it wasn't the correct thing to do.

One evening, my parents went out to an event at Fort Leonard Wood, and I was left at home with a teenaged female babysitter who was the daughter of our landlord. During the time my parents were out, the young babysitter decided that I, at age 5, could still help her out sexually. I was molested. At the time I didn't understand what was happening, but I knew I didn't like it. When my parents returned, they asked me if I was okay. I was shy about answering and they could sense something was wrong, so they kept asking questions to get at what happened. Mom and Dad were very upset, and Mom charged out of the house to the babysitter's duplex near ours. When no one was home, she decided to go the landlord's general store across the road the next morning.

When the store opened, she picked me up in her arms, still upset from the night before, and we crossed the dangerous highway. Upon entering the store Mom blasted the babysitter and her mother, who were standing behind the counter. I don't remember what she said, Mom didn't use profanity but if she had, I think the word slut would have been brought up several times. I felt Mom's anger and became angry as well. I remember wanting to do something to show my anger but found I was too emotional to speak so I knocked a box of Jell-O off a nearby shelf. With Mom satisfied that she had made her point, we left the store. I don't know if Dad told the military authorities on base about the incident. If he had and they decided to classify the rental houses off limits, that would have prevented any military personnel from renting them, causing a big financial blow to the landlord. What I do know is that after a couple of months we were transferred out of Fort Leonard Wood to Fort Knox, our second tour there.

Fort Knox was a good post for our family. I was in my fifth to seventh years of life. Our house was an eight-foot-wide trailer, and it was on-base housing—no snakes or bad babysitters to worry about.

To supplement our limited income, Mom took a job waiting tables at the Officers Club on base. That was a plus because not only did she, and we, have more money, but she got to hear and meet celebrity entertainers such as Woody Herman and his orchestra. Mom also participated in a Jantzen swimsuit contest where the top two ladies were asked to pose for a photo shoot, Mom was one of the top two, and I still have the photos. The only thing negative that happened at Fort Knox was one hot summer day when I was playing with friends and we were horsing around, pushing, and shoving one of the kid's Irish Setter decided I was being too aggressive and bit me on the ear. I went home, blood flowing, and ended up at the base hospital for a couple of stitches. Unfortunately, military regulations required the dog to be euthanized after rabies testing. The dog didn't have rabies, and I felt horrible for causing its death.

Our last year at Fort Knox I wanted a toy drum set for Christmas. Each place we lived, my parents tried to make it our home, with as few restrictions as possible, but in this case, Mom was in favor of my request and Dad was against it. I was pleased that Mom won the debate, and I got my beloved drum set. I banged on it driving my parents crazy until I hit the snare drum too hard and punctured the batter head, and since there were no replacement parts available, it was the end of my drumming at that time.

Coming back to the reality of our flight to Paris as we were ending our thirteen-hour flight and landing at Orly Airport outside of Paris. We deplaned and headed for the Immigration Checkpoint. First, there were long lines. Then there were stern stares from the Immigrations Officer, bordering on intimidation. Then came the questions, "So, Mrs. Kirk, why are you coming to our country? How Long will you be staying? … Where will you be staying?" The stern stares continued, along with long pauses, before the Officer stamped our passport and we could proceed to collect luggage and go through Customs. I say our passport because at that time and given my age Mom and I shared a passport containing a photo of the two of us. Once we collected our luggage, we presented the French Entry form, a lengthy form that had to be filled out on the plane before landing, with any declarations noted. We presented the form to the Customs Officer, and they decided if our luggage would be opened and searched. They gave the impression that if we had something in our luggage that we shouldn't have, we would be put in jail, so luckily, we weren't searched.

While we were going through the formal entry process into France, I was carrying a secret in my pocket. Before we departed for Paris, mom sold our Buick Roadmaster, and I was carrying the proceeds. It was illegal to carry large sums of U.S. currency into France and I had a couple of thousand dollars in my pockets. My parents reasoned that as a small child, I wouldn't be scrutinized and could get away with carrying it into the country, and it worked. We made it past the hurdles without ending up in a French jail and we could finally reunite with Dad. I was eager to give him the money in my pocket, but he wasn't eager for me to show him my secret in the airport. Later, in the airport parking lot, I gave Dad the money and my smuggling career was over for the time being.

Dad had purchased a dark blue Simca, a small French car for us to use while in France. The car reminded me of a small version of the 1940's Ford's or Chevrolet's. Its unique characteristic was that, in cold weather, ice formed on the inside of the windshield as well as the outside. We loaded the luggage and got into the car for our trip to our new home in Metz, France.

The trip to Metz was wondrous. My eyes kept going from left to right at the new sights and sounds of the picturesque French countryside. Since the weather was mild, the car windows were open bringing ever-changing and intriguing smells into the car. This sensory stimulation only increased my delight and anticipation.

After a three-and-a-half-hour drive, we arrived in Metz a small-town a little over three hundred kilometers northeast of Paris at the junction of the Moselle and Seile rivers and near the German border. The recorded history of Metz goes back before 52 B.C. and has been a part of Germany or France at various times and I learned that just over ten years before, the U.S. Third Army led by General George S. Patton had fought, a difficult battle in Metz; this battle was a key part of the U.S.'s drive north into Germany. As a child, I was interested in the history, or the history being made in the places where I've visited or lived.

Dad had selected a two-bedroom flat on the second floor of a farmhouse outside of Metz. The house was painted white with green wooden shutters and built from concrete and stone. It was striking against the rolling farmland and green vegetation. The internal layout of the house was such that the rooms on the first floor and second floor weren't separated. There was an open staircase, meaning that all second-floor individual rooms opened into a common landing and staircase. I didn't mind the arrangement, but with us occupying the second floor and the French owners living on the first floor, Mom wasn't pleased with our lack of privacy and this lack of privacy became unsettling, even for me.

I was happy that they had children about my age whom I enjoyed playing with every day. I didn't speak French, and they didn't speak English. However, language differences didn't pose a problem, with hand gestures, facial expressions, and each of us learning a few words and learning that you can communicate even if you don't know the other person's language. It only takes trying.

Mom was a strong-minded person who wanted what she felt was best for her family and had two issues with the flat. First, it was out of town, away from the military commissary, shopping, and other facilities and since there was no public transportation that far out, we had to rely on the one car, which Dad took to work. The second was the lack of a door separating us from the first floor. These two issues made Mom increasingly unhappy until one day, "Jim, you must find us another place to live" Mom said. My dad's first name is James and when Mom used the emphasized Jim, it meant he needed to listen. That brief conversation inspired

Dad to seek other accommodations. He did, and we moved into town within three months. But our moving so quickly also made the farmhouse owners unhappy. They thought they were going to have renter's income for a period of two years, and now, after three months we were moving, which cost us a two-month rent penalty. The flat in town was smaller with a single kitchen and living room combination but it did have two bedrooms, and one bathroom. And it had Mom's two requirements, a proper door out to our apartment, and it was closer to military facilities, with public transportation as an option.

Neither the first nor second flat had a refrigerator. The custom, at that time, in France was to shop for perishable food daily, a custom we Americans weren't used to following. We weren't allowed to shop on the French economy, so we had to buy our food at the military commissary. Picking up perishable food at the commissary every day wasn't possible, even with the improved transportation options. I believe some Americans disregarded the rules and bought items locally. Also, a refrigerator was impossible to get which leads me to the blue milk and ice chunks issue. The commissary milk had a blue tint because it came from a powdered milk formula. The ice chunks were present because we put the milk outside on the kitchen windowsill. In cold weather the milk would freeze. Corn flakes with blue ice milk—a "special" treat—was a shock to my system each morning.

While living in Metz my parent decided we would visit friends stationed in Germany for the long weekend. The drive north took us through the city of Saarbrucken. At the time, Saarbrucken was a French protectorate in transition, after a referendum vote, to the Federal Republic of Germany. As we drove through the city, we became entangled in a worker's demonstration. Like May Day was adopted in 1889 by the communist and socialist as International Worker's Day, workers demonstrations about the cause du jour pop up periodically. Our car was required to have a U.S. Forces license plate, about the size of a French plate with a black background, white lettering, and French foreign forces designation of 2 CF on the left side of the plate. It stood out from the European plates and was easy for the demonstrators to see and know we were Americans.

Once the crowd saw our plates we were targeted for attack. We could see them pointing at us and starting to run our way. "Get us out of here" yelled Mom. "I will, don't worry" replied Dad.

I was alarmed and confused because of my parents' elevated voices, concern, and a large crowd headed our way. Dad immediately turned into another street, but another crowd was coming down that one, so he took another turn only to run into a third crowd. It was as if they were all converging, possibly headed for the town square. As the last crowd got closer, they started throwing objects at our car. Because of the car's thin metal and zero insulation, each time an object hit the car, it sounded like a cannon had gone off inside. When the crowd got to us, they started rocking the car back and forth. With the objects hitting the car along with the crowd's yelling produced a defining noise. I was panicked and was unsure as to what was about to happen. The rocking of the car made it feel as though we were going on our side. Finally, Dad was able to get enough tire traction on the pavement to accelerate and get us out of the chaos. Once we felt safe, Mom and Dad had a lengthy argument about why we "got lost," who was to blame, and why we didn't know that Americans shouldn't travel in locations where scheduled workers demonstrations were being held. But I was happy that we were on our way to Germany. This incident points up the face that homework and situational awareness are vital.

Our stay in Metz was a short seven months, and I don't remember much more than going to school, our apartment, and the blue milk. While in Metz I attended the Department of Defense dependent school[1], but I searched and couldn't find a Metz school picture. That means I probably wasn't present when the photos were taken. This is a common occurrence when you are an Army brat and constantly moving.

---

[1] US DoDDS

CHAPTER 2

HAPPINESS & HORROR

After our brief time in Metz, Dad received orders to go to Munich, Germany. This was wonderful news; our family was excited because Munich offered a far superior quality of life. We could even have a refrigerator. However, it did mean Dad had to extend his tour of duty in Europe by another year.

By Christmas, we were in our military-provided housing and preparing for a new year. Our new housing, named Perlacher Forest[2], was in a U.S. military community, which had, schools, a hospital, a movie theater, and sports fields. It was almost totally self-contained and an oasis of Americana, absent the PX and Commissary. However, the PX and Commissary were conveniently located on the military base, McGraw Kaserne[3], a mile and a half from our housing. In addition to our flat, the Military provided furniture, cookware, plates, utensils, and linens. All we had to do was move our clothing in and buy food. Our building was a three-story apartment complex with three stair wells consisting of six apartments each, a basement, which extended the length of the building, contained storage units for each apartment, and a large recreation room in the attic above each stair well. The recreation rooms were great for those days when the weather was bad. The stair well entrance was between the basement and the first apartment level. We had the apartment in the middle stair well first level on the right. In that location, it felt I was in the center of anything going on outside. I've always had

---

[2] Perlacher Forest - A forested area near Munich
[3] Kaserne - German for garrison or barracks

a strong desire to be where things are happening. In the summer and on weekends, I would awake the second I heard any activity outside, immediately dress and go out to join in. I felt a sense of freedom and security in this new home, and I could ride my bike everywhere, often to school.

Up to this point in my life, I hadn't lived in a multi-family apartment complex or place that had a high concentration of people. I had lived in Metz and on bases, but they were in single family homes or buildings with one other family. Perlacher Forests Housing was different, I noticed the military personnel and their dependents created a more diverse family makeup, differences in country of origin, cultures, race, religion, and first language. This new environment turned out to be a lasting positive learning experience. Dinner time meant wonderfully rich smells in the stair well of our building coming from the many ethnic foods being prepared. The smells of Italian red sauce with garlic, Asian spicy fish soup, Southern US fried chicken, German sausages and sauerkraut, Middle Eastern foods with a myriad of spices, French escargot with garlic and butter along with aromatic cheeses and breads, and some dishes I couldn't identify that made my mouth water, I wanted to try all of them. On occasion I did get to enjoy some of these tasty meals thanks to our friendly neighbors.

Living in this community reminded me of my introduction to France and how I could communicate, play with, and like people even with our differences.

My father encouraged me to join the ROA, Reserve Officers Association's, little league baseball team. This was one of many teams formed in our development and the games were played on our neighborhood ball fields. My baseball skills were mixed. I was good at fielding—I played left field—but needed <u>major</u> work when it came to batting. "Kirk, just get on base," my coach would plead, I did get on base from time to time by trickery.

I would crouch lower than normal in the batter's box and doing other hijinks to throw off the pitcher's rhythm. At some point in each game the plate umpire would tell me to stop or else. "Kid, cut it out" the umpires would say. In Little League we're to learn the fundamentals of baseball, work on rules of the game, its etiquette, and muscle memory. However, our team was good enough to win a championship, not just a participation trophy.

My friends and I liked to venture out of the community to the nearby Perlacher forests. The forest had tall trees with the branches cut off all the way to near the top. The forest floor was clean with little undergrowth, mostly pine needles lay on the ground. There was a strong smell of pine and moss—clean, refreshing, and healthy. The high forest canopy blocked out some sunlight which made the forest dark inside. As I walked through it, I could see rays of sunlight piercing the canopy like arrows. The forest was a good place to play hide and seek or just enjoying the surroundings, it made me feel calm and peaceful.

Another favorite activity was the movies, and I especially liked the Saturday Matinee. Dad moonlighted at the military base theater, which meant that I could get into this theater before anyone else and didn't have to pay the quarter price to see the Saturday Matinee. I felt like Mr. Cool. The Matinee was a fun way to meet my friends and enjoy hanging out for hours, eating popcorn, watching movies like The Lone Ranger—*False Accusations*, Sky King—*The Plastic Ghost*, and Roy Rogers—*Horse Crazy*. The cartoons were great with a whole series of titles that included Woody Woodpecker, Mighty Mouse, and Crusader Rabbit. Over time movies became my refuge and as an only child I could get lost in them.

Dad was dedicated to our family's welfare and if that meant a second job, he always found a way, working at the base theater, Officers Club or even buying American cars from fellow G.I.'s fixing them up and reselling them. Mom volunteered at the military hospital located within the housing complex. It was a volunteer job because American military dependents weren't permitted to work for pay—those jobs were reserved for country nationals. She had always worked, and this volunteer job gave her an opportunity to learn dental assistant skills—she would use those skills many times again back in the States. It was a normal life with two parents working, only Dad worked longer hours, and I missed him being around in the evenings. They both were my role models for work ethic.

Sometimes I would join my parents at the Enlisted Club, a club for non-officer ranks, on family night. The club was, as you would expect, a dining area, a bar area (you had to be eighteen to enter), and a stage area. The family night consisted of dinner and usually, live entertainment. Mom and Dad got steak or chicken, and occasionally Dad would get the fish since he was the only one in our family who liked fish. I stuck with my usual hamburger, fries, and Coke. The entertainment was always great because it's a tradition that various entertainment celebrities tour the military installations around the world to entertain the troops. On one occasion, I met Louis Armstrong, and he even sat down at our table for a couple of minutes to say hello. His performance was an incredible experience and afterward, Mom and Dad explained in more detail who he was. This was my first encounter with jazz, and when possible, I listening to him on the Armed Forces Network (AFN) Radio which exposed me to other jazz musicians. That was the beginning of my love for jazz. The network played many different types of music from classical to rock n' roll which expanded my musical appreciation. However, each genre was only played at a specific time of the day so if I wanted rock n' roll I had to tune in at that time or not hear it until the next day.

I loved living in Munich and felt comfortable yet exhilarated when visiting museums, art galleries, parks, cafes, and tasting the Bavarian cuisine. I loved the food; I still do and will get it whenever I can. The typical Bavarian restaurant is an

Austrian-German architecture combination, a variation on the farmhouse or chalet. The external walls are usually a concrete mixture of sand and limestone brick masonry called Kalksandsteinmauerwerk[4] and are painted white or off white with plenty of wood inside and out as well as big garden areas. Sitting in the garden with the warm sun shining and eating robust food is a wonderful experience, an example is the well-known German beer garden, Biergarten. But in parts of Germany, they have the apple wine gardens, or Apfelwein gardens. Later, during my consulting life, I was a victim of drinking apple wine in a sunny garden without cutting it with fifty percent water, as most locals do. The result was a bad headache the next morning. I especially love the potato dishes, Kartoffel. German cottage potatoes, fried potatoes, potato salad, and potato pancakes to name a few. Meat dishes like Wienerschnitzle, Bratwurst, Bockwurst, and Frankfurter Sausage are also favorites. The breads are exceptional—Semmels, Pretzels, and Volkornbrot. These foods are, for me, comfort foods, although they can be a bit heavy.

Our first Christmas in Munich was a magical time. Our family's first order of business was to get a Christmas tree and decorate our apartment. When Saturday came for us to buy our tree, I jumped out of bed, quickly dressed and was ready to go in minutes. We went to the PX on base and walked up and down the line of trees for sale until we found the one, we all liked. At the check-out we were given instructions on safety and how to get the tree sprayed with fire retardant. The only issue was that the mandatory military place to get the tree sprayed wouldn't open again until Monday. The disappointment I felt was overwhelming. I was so excited about getting the tree and getting it up in our apartment only to have to wait until at least Monday was unthinkable. Dad would have to go back to the PX, pick up the tree and stand in line to get it sprayed, and then bring it home, all while trying to do his day and evening jobs on base. There was no

---

[4] Kalksandsteinmauerwerk - Sand & Lime Bricks

option—military rules are inflexible. We did get the tree up Monday night and our Christmas celebration continued.

Another favorite part of Christmas was going to the small shops in the Munich city center on Christmas Eve, walking the narrow streets with light snow falling searching for the right "Santa's workshop" to find the gifts I wanted to buy. My gift list contained presents for my parents and for an American family we were to visit for New Year's. I was given a certain amount of money to find and buy the gifts I wanted to give for Christmas. That amount of money was fixed, no exceptions. On this occasion I searched, found, and purchased blown-glass gifts consisting of a figurine of an elk, mixed drink stirs, and a flower from a local artist for Mom and Dad. I also purchased a box for assorted chocolates for our American friends. The rest of our families Christmas presents were purchased from the Sears, Roebuck and Company catalog. This meant we had to order gifts early to ensure delivery. We did, however, purchase a few things at the Post Exchange. Our Christmas was one of the best even with the tree issues.

After Christmas we traveled to Wiesbaden which is a four-hour drive to visit our American friends. On New Year's Eve our friends opened my gift and began eating the chocolates. It was at that time we all discovered the chocolates were filled with liqueur. I was embarrassed because our friends didn't drink any type of spirits, and they were feeling the effects. With the adults feeling a little tipsy there were a lot of laughs. It was heartwarming to see our friends but we had to return to Munich the following day so my parents could get back to work.

Munich in the southeastern part of Germany, in the State of Bavaria. It's close to Switzerland and Austria. The U.S. military operated a recreational area in Garmisch-Partenkirchen. These two towns, which were united in 1935, are nestled in a valley with beautiful mountains, rivers, and breathtaking views. The military hotels in the recreational area were less expensive than those on the open market, and since they were within our budget, we took advantage of that and vacationed there several times.

I enjoyed the Alps and climbing the midrange high mountains because being on them offered a view of the valleys that was both expansive and beautiful. The winter months there was skiing on the fantastic slops. On one of our trips, during the summer months, I tried sliding down the same slops on what was then the exposed loose flat shale rock base. Doing this meant that when I got to the bottom, my tennis shoes were in shreds. Of course I got into serious trouble, I didn't try that again. I did have a chance to visit Mount Zugspitze by railway and cable car on one of our vacation trips. At Mount Zugspitze, you are standing above the clouds where the air is pure, the views went on forever, and the panorama is breathtaking. To this day I still love being on top of a mountain with the cool clean air where all you see is blue sky, mighty summits, and breathtaking vastness. My appreciation of our world and its beauty was ignited and still burns hot.

The schools in Munich were much better than Metz. Even though both schools were run by the U.S. Department of Defense, I believe the difference was the teaching staff. The level of competition for teachers to get the Munich assignments was greater, and therefore the skills were higher, or it could've been I was just happier in Munich than Metz. It was required that I take German in school, a language I enjoyed learning. The only sad thing about learning a language is the level of fluency goes away without frequent reinforcement. My German and French—a little was learned in Metz but more later when I lived in Paris—does come back when I'm in Germany or France, where I can read and hear the familiar words again. The lesson here is, like any skill: you keep it fresh, or you lose it.

The Germans in Munich, like the French in Metz, were friendly, and during our stay in Germany, many became close friends. In those days, ten years after WWII, the economy was still recovering. The German Mark to U.S. Dollar exchange rate was four to one—not bad for us when we made purchases in the local market. We exchanged our dollars for Marks on base to pay for the goods we bought, because Germans weren't allowed to have U.S. dollars, or the U.S. military printed "Script," which was like Monopoly money. Even with these rules, some Germans had obtained both U.S. dollars and Script. Periodically the U.S. Military would change out the old Script for new which would send the Germans holding the old Script into a frenzy. They would approach U.S. personnel and ask to get help exchanging their Script for the new, which was illegal, and some would make the exchange for a fraction of the old Script's value. We could convert dollars to marks for our purchases, but we had another alternative. The currency challenges led to a thriving barter market, or some would call it a black market. I remember one guy came to our door selling Coca Cola. We could get Coke at the U.S. commissary, but my dad chose to trade for it because this guy was a former German Soldier. My Dad was the type of person who made friends quickly and it wasn't long before they were exchanging stories. Both had received wounds during the war, a common bond, each jokingly accusing the other of inflicting their wounds. When I said trade that meant we could buy things in our Post Exchange and Commissary that the Germans couldn't get or were expensive. Dad would buy things that his gentleman wanted in exchange for the Coca Cola he sold. What I learned from my father actions is that I can still be friends with someone who I didn't like, with different philosophies, or even fought against.

During our time in Germany, Mom and Dad taught me many life lessons at a time when I needed this guidance and knowledge. For example: How to keep my clothes and appearance sharp, what was honorable when interacting with others, why it's important to have values and not stray from them, why family is essential, and why I should stand up when greeting elders. Mom taught me about etiquette and how to respect girls. Throughout my life I've learned a lot of great things from my parents, and I'm sad they're no longer alive. I can also say that I've slipped from time to time and haven't always managed to stay one hundred percent true to these values, something I've regretted each time. I can say once you have learned them, it's easier to go back to them. The lesson for me is that it's a hard day to day out challenge and you can't give up. I've also learned that when something is supposed to happen, it will. When something isn't supposed to happen, roadblocks will be thrown in your way, and it will be difficult to proceed. I try to listen more and reevaluate the path I'm taking. That doesn't mean to back off when things get tough—it means be sure It's the right path.

Not everything in Munich was positive. Espionage flourished between the U.S. and Soviets after the WWII and Munich was one of the hotbeds in Germany. I remember a young nice French lady, who was occasionally my sitter, and always brought me a present, like a wooden or metal car, truck, or airplane. I also remember that U.S. soldiers would visit her while Mom and Dad were out, but I didn't care since I was playing with my new toy. After sitting with me a few times, the U.S. Army investigators visited us to ask my parents and me about this lady. She was reportedly a Soviet spy, of course the lady could no longer work for us, and we never knew what happened to her after that day.

I had another encounter, after Ft. Leonard Wood, of people being abusive. It was on a rainy weekend when a few other kids in our building and I were playing in the top floor recreation room. For some unknown reason one kids, known to be a bully, started to berate another one who had cerebral palsy. I told the bully to stop, "Mind your own business" he said to me with a menacing look in his eyes and kept up his verbal attack. At that point I was enraged at the abuse, so I got up, grabbed the bully, pushed him out the recreation room door and into the stairwell, which was partially open three floors down to the basement, where I hung his head over the side. "I told you to stop, you are now going to experience the feeling of helpless," I said. After a few seconds, I let him go and told him to go home and not come back. It only took about ten minutes, when I heard him and his older bigger brother shouting from their end of the basement stairwell. The basement walkway was open from the first stairwell to the third stairwell and sounds carried. I went down to the basement to confront them but, it turned out to be a shouting match with the bully and his brother at their end and me at mine, they finally retreated to their apartment. My takeaway was it's okay to confront abuse, but not necessarily to hang bullies over a stairwell.

Much more atrocious than encountering a bully was Dachau. The first of Hitler's concentration camps, which operated from March 1933 until April 1945 and was about fifteen miles or a forty-minute drive northwest of Munich. There an estimated 200,000 prisoners processed and housed during the time it was operating. Of those prisoners there were between 32,000 and 41,500 documented deaths. When we lived in Munich the authorities were still investigating and turning up new evidence in the camp. News was shared about the horrific findings from time to time. It was disturbing, and I had trouble understanding how these things could've happened.

We weren't permitted to go to Dachau to see what had gone on while the investigations were being conducted. However, many years later, a younger business colleague and I were on a project in Frankfurt and took the weekend off to visit Munich. On our way back to Frankfurt I asked my colleague if we could stop at Dachau. I had to explain what it was since he had limited knowledge of concentration camps and hadn't heard of Dachau. As we drove to Dachau, the seriousness of my explanation had not sunk in, and he was still his usual jovial self. When we arrived at the front gates, he wanted a video recording "this adventure," as he said. We first went into the information center where there were artifacts, photos, and stories from the camp. We saw many lists of prisoners' entries to the camp, lists of their personal items seized, prisoner identification records and their photos, lists of deaths, detail records on cremation "production," photos of pole hangings, dead bodies, camp facilities and a short documentary film on the camp. The horrors of what had happened started to sink in. Next, we took the guided tour of the camp, which was being restored to its 1945 condition. We saw the prisoner quarters where bunks were stacked high with little separation from bunk to bunk. It was dark inside and with the density of bunks it felt oppressive and spartan.

After the barracks, we went to the gas chamber building. We entered the building and then into the chamber itself, a small room painted white with a low ceiling, with my height of six feet, I could easily touch the ceiling. The guide described the step-by-step procedure of the prisoner selection and movement into the chamber. Then, the heavy metal door behind us was swung and slammed shut with chilling effect. I started to feel claustrophobic and wanted to leave. I was looking around the room when the guide called our attention to a small grate in the center of the ceiling above where I was standing. This is where the guards dropped the poisonous gas pellets that would kill their prisoners. I was nauseous to think of people standing in my spot that had died. As if viewing the gas chamber wasn't enough, we next went to the ovens. Photos we had seen earlier of bodies in the ovens came rushing back in my mind. The guide said the ovens had been continuously in use after their construction and additional ovens were frequently being built but they couldn't keep up with the number of dead bodies. The photo's showed bodies were stacked up, like logs, near the ovens waiting to be cremated. We finished the tour, and my friend asked me if he could be alone for a while. I walked away to give him space. I needed space as well because the horrors of what I had heard all these years and what I saw here hit me hard.

On our way out through the gates, he asked me to video him, he wanted to capture his feelings and thoughts. His statement reflected a changed person, a somber person. He talked about his sorrow and didn't understand how this could happen. He asked how the people in the nearby village hadn't known of this place. I saw some guilt in his eyes for not knowing the story before. Our ride back to Frankfurt was a quiet one. We both knew there were bad people in the world and even worse people who are cruel when seeking power, but it takes the rest of us to say *no*!

Two additional events, while we lived in Munich, which has stayed with me, were the 1956 Hungarian Revolution and the 1956 Poznan Poland Protests.

The workers in Poznan, Poland's largest factory went on strike in June 1956, to protest the Soviet Union controlled Polish government and the problems in the Poznan factory. Those issues were productivity quotas, health and safety concerns, and low wages. By noon on that day approximately one hundred thousand people were protesting around the government buildings. The Polish People's Army suppressed the demonstration by firing on the protesting civilians. The result was hundreds of casualties and arrests in the weeks that followed the strike, and refugees fleeing Poland.

In Hungary the Revolution, also known as the "uprising", started in Budapest in November 1956, with university students protesting the USSR's geopolitical domination of Hungary. After entered the Hungarian Radio building to broadcast their sixteen demands for political and economic reforms, the delegation was detained. When protesters outside the Radio building demanded their release, police from the state protection authority shot and killed several protestors. That initial confrontation grew into a countrywide revolution against the Hungarian Stalinist government and the domestic policies imposed by the USSR. Hungarian militias and anti-communist political prisoners released from prison acquired arms and proceeded to fight against local Communist leaders and police. After initial negotiations broke down the USSR rolled tanks into Hungary and put down the revolution after six days of fighting. The impact on people's lives was devastating with 2,500 Hungarians and 700 Soviet Army soldiers killed, and 200,000 Hungarian refugees fleeing the country.

The flood of refugees from both events had an impact on Western Europe, the United Kingdom, and we saw the impact in Munich. Refugees have migrated for hundreds of years and rely on other people and governments for assistance. In Germany the U.S. military was the primary provider of food, clothing, and shelter to the refugees. Almost all the refugees were grateful to be leaving the conflict in their country, even though they missed their homes, their everyday lives, some even left their families, but they were appreciative of the help provided. I did hear a few stories of selfishness by a small number of refugees demanding more than what could be provided. I can try to grasp the trauma of being displaced from your homeland, the violence, and oppression they experienced, but selfishness I don't understand. If someone is trying to help you, why demand more? Demand more stylish clothes, different food, different cosmetics, and other items they were used to having at home or expected from a more affluent country. History tells of an untold number of refugees who have gone on to build new and successful lives in their adopted countries without displaying this degree of self-centeredness

CHAPTER 3

COMING HOME

When it came time to leave Germany, in the summer of 1959, I was both sad to leave the great life we had and my friends, but excited to get back to the U.S.A. As before, we flew on a TWA Super Connie with the two refueling stops. The difference this time was that I didn't get sick on the plane and monopolize the rest rooms like I had on the flight to Europe. We landed at New York's Idlewild Airport and took a cab to a specified car dealership where we were picking up our new four-door hard top Pontiac Bonneville, ordered through our Post Exchange on base in Munich. That process took a while to complete, but we finally started out on our trip, driving to Fort Rucker, Alabama, our next duty assignment.

Fort Rucker is in the lower eastern corner of Alabama. It's approximately eighty miles south of Montgomery, twenty miles northwest of Dothan and eighty miles north of the Florida Gulf Coast. Other communities near the base are Enterprise, Daleville, and Ozark. It sits in the East Gulf Costal Plan in what is called the Wiregrass section because of the trough grass that once grew in the area. The terrain varies throughout the area, and it has a strong history of being a farming community. Fort Rucker is an Army Aviation training base focusing on helicopters. At that time the Army was assembling, and testing attached machine guns and rockets on the helicopters. Troops were constantly making canvas and wood framed tanks, jeeps, trucks, and other items used for targets on the firing range. While driving through the base it looked comical to see men lifting and moving these targets around.

The trip to Alabama took two days and at the end of the first day we stopped at a Howard Johnson's restaurant for dinner. One of the meals that I had missed and wanted as soon as I could get it was a Howard Johnson's hot roast beef sandwich. My anticipation grew as we got closer to the restaurant. Once we pulled up to the restaurant I rushed inside to order and eat my desired treat. The plate came open-faced with white bread, mashed potatoes, deli-style roast beef and thick dark brown beef gravy. Oh, there was some corn on the side as well, but it didn't capture my attention. I ate every delicious bite, and it seemed like I inhale the meal. Afterward I felt a bit sick, probably because it was considerably richer than the food I was used to eating in my day-to-day routine in Germany. Where meals eaten in the military facilities, snack bars, Post Exchange, and school cafeteria were bland, requiring salt and pepper to have any taste at all. At home mom usually cooked meat and potatoes, and occasionally a vegetable, all tasty, but not as rich as the hot roast beef sandwich with gravy.

An example of the on base food was the vegetables which were cooked in water and served from a pot of water on a steam table. By the time it was served, there was no taste and probably no nutritional value, just green and yellow wax tasting items on the plate. I blame this for the reason I continue to put salt and pepper on food before I taste it, a habit I've worked to quit. Nevertheless, I got my Howard Johnson's treat. It did feel good to be back in the United States, and home. I've always considered the entire United States as my home because most of my life was living on or near military assignments and local communities. I only visited family birthplaces a few times.

Upon arrival my dad reported in and was told that his job assignment, hadn't been vacated, which meant he was reassigned to the Finance and Accounting unit who did have an immediate vacancy. Dad had been Armor/Infantry for his entire military career, and this was a total switch in skill set. In those days the military would reassign people based on vacancies, and they tried to stay within the person's skill set, but that didn't always happen. The positive was that the Army started his training immediately in the new world of computers. I don't remember the specific model of the UNIVAC mainframe he worked on, but it was in the days when boards had to be wired to make the machine do want was required.

As with dad's job assignment our on-base housing wasn't available when we arrived either, the housing office recommended a rental property in Daleville, Alabama until on-base housing was ready. Of course, no timeframe was given. The summer months in southeast Alabama are hot and muggy, while the winters are cold, and it's wet and partly cloudy year-round. When we arrived, the temperatures were in the nineties with a humidity in the upper nineties—as opposed to that of Munich, Germany where the temperature in the summer were in the mid-sixties with seventy percent humidity and moderate rain. Moving to south Alabama in the middle of summer from the cooler climate of Germany, was brutal enough. But the house we rented was without air conditioning. It was a simple two bedroom with one bath and living-dining-kitchen combo which suited our needs. For some reason, which I never found out, mom wasn't comfortable leaving our windows open at night. When dusk came, we shut the windows until after dawn the next day, without the cooler night air as a break from the heat.

Mom, a person who is aggressive and gets results, while being polite and respectful, went to the base housing office every day to ask about the status of our base housing. I do mean every day she sat in their office for several hours. It only took a couple of weeks, and we were given base housing with air conditioning. My lesson from her was that I can push to get results and be polite at the same time.

The move on base offered another positive—we bought a television. Coming back to the United States after Germany was the first time, at eleven years old, I had a television in my house. We had a radio in both France and Germany but no television. One news program I remember watching on television in January 1960. was Castro's one year anniversary of the takeover in Cuba from the Batista government. Batista was friendly toward the U.S. and the question; would Castro be as well? Since Cuba is so close to the U.S. would Castro's coming to power have a security impact on us. Castro had visited the U.S. in April of 1959, just after taking over in January, and while he was the hero of many Americans, he was cold towards the U.S. government. The TV commentators speculated on different scenarios. The prevalent projection, however, was that Castro would be anti-U.S. and pro-Soviet Union. As 1960 progressed Castro became increasingly agitated with the U.S. and openly accused them of trying to interfere in Cuba's future. His feelings became apparent when in September of 1960 he addressed the United Nations with a tone of defiance. That was the beginning of a long adversarial history with the Castro government. It was exciting to see change in the world but, to have an apparent pro-communist government so close to the United States was unsettling. That brought back memories the 1956 brutality in Hungary and Poland and the ongoing cold war with the Soviet Union since WWII.

In July of 1959 U.S. Vice President Richard Nixon and Soviet Premier Nikita Khrushchev met in Moscow, during the opening of the American National Exhibition, for what was called the "Kitchen Debate." My hopes were that this was a small beginning to thaw the cold war.

However, in March of 1960, U.S. President Dwight D. Eisenhower signed off on the National Security Council directive on anti-Cuban covert action. The Council recognized that the USSR and Communist China, along with their puppet governments and groups, were engaging in covert actions therefore authorizing the United States to supplement their overt activities with covert operations. The CIA ran covert operations including the attempted assignation of Castro and President Kennedy approved the failed Bay of Pigs Invasion. These and other U.S. Policies have continued the continuous situation with Cuba.

Another event happened in February of 1960. The Greensboro, N.C. Woolworth lunch counter sit-in began a process, for many, of uncomfortable change. As we know, change requires discomfort. However, at the time this was something I noticed but didn't take an active role in observing or understanding the change.

Ten months later, we were just getting settled when dad was assigned as military advisor assignment to an Army Reserve Unit in Asheville, N.C. Dad wouldn't get back to his job in computers with the Army until several years later. Asheville was a big change from hot and sandy Fort Rucker and clearly deserved its nick name of "Land in the Sky." It's located at the southernmost part of the Blue Ridge Mountains in Western N.C. where the plant life from the Southeast, Northeast, and Mid-West converge. The diversity of nourishing soil, in the Appalachian temperate rainforest (one of only two in the U.S.), and its natural irrigation create a unique place for fantastic flora. Today, Asheville is also known for its vibrant arts scene, great restaurants, tourist attractions such as the Biltmore Estates, outdoor activities including camping, hiking, mountain climbing, and whitewater kayaking.

Moving to Asheville was my first true experience living in a place that wasn't close to a military base. For me it was another time of growth. I was twelve when we moved to Asheville and sixteen when we left. Our first house was in West Asheville and a rental. West Asheville was a normal, working-class neighborhood and close to Dad's work. The house was a two-bedroom, one bath with kitchen and living room. We did have a small basement where the car took up most of the space. Our source of heat was an oil system with a large single duct in the hallway floor. That meant the hallway was hot, and the house extremities weren't. Our family lived in this house for a year until Mom and Dad bought a new house in Oteen, on the outskirts of Asheville where we lived for the rest of our time there. The new house had a combination living and dining room, two bedrooms and one bath and a carport for the car. The lot was huge and took me a while to mow every other week. It grew fast because Dad had gotten a truck load of chicken manure to spread on the lawn for fertilizer. The smell was horrible for a few weeks until the manure was absorbed into the earth.

My first school in West Asheville was different from my U.S. DoDDS in Munich. Most of what was being taught I had already had in Germany except for having to take North Carolina history. This time however, my family didn't have to buy my books like we did in Alabama. This was my realization that the various states had their own unique way of doing things. Later in my educational life I would learn more about the rights of the U.S. States versus the roll of the U.S Federal Government. Overall, the school year was easy and uneventful. With our move to Oteen I had to change schools to a new middle school closer to our house and in a more affluent part of town. This school and the advancement in grade level felt different. It seemed far more competitive and confrontational but still behind my former U.S. DoDDS in Munich.

Mom, had taken a job as a dental assistant and because of her dental assistant background, wanted the best dental care for our family. One of the first things she did was make an appointment for me to see her dentist and ask about getting braces since orthodontic care wasn't available to dependents in Munich. Of course, after seeing the dentist I was referred to an orthodontist. Mom asked how long it would take for my teeth to straighten and the treatment completed. She was used to us moving frequently and wanted my treatment to be completed before we had to ship out. As it turned out, it took a year, and we were still living in Asheville. For me, the treatment wasn't fun. I usually went to the orthodontist on Fridays for my adjustments and my ritual after words was to get a large bag of puffed Cheetos and some Coca-Cola which would dissolve the Cheetos—That was my evening meal since my mouth was too sore for anything else.

I almost immediately came face to face with a new encounter, criticism about my clothing. I wore clothing from the military Post Exchange [5] which was blousy khaki pants and usually a patterned shirt. To me this was normal since I had lived on or around military bases, but to my classmates I wasn't wearing the acceptable or "in" things. Having braces didn't improve my status in school, it was considered something nerds did. I began to feel inadequate and that I didn't belong in the civilian world.

I realized that my sheltered life to date was over. The things my age group liked and disliked, and this civilian world overall were different. While the ordeal continued through the year in this school, I realized that I had better get up to speed on the differences, especially fashion. Even though I had adapted to other languages and cultures before, I needed to understand this new world. So, I began to visit the local men's shops and the college men's shops to see what was the "in" things to wear. By the second year I started the transition to wearing more stylish and acceptable clothes—at least, as much as my parents could afford. Even having braces was now acceptable. I continued my fashion education the whole time in Asheville. With summer jobs and a lawn mowing service I was able to increase my wardrobe without relying on them. My improved and acceptable wardrobe consisted of trim khaki pants, preppy shirts with matching socks, preppy belt, and Bass Weejuns for a start.

---

[5] Post Exchange - PX a military department store

Being an Army Brat, as we call ourselves, I had to adapt fit in wherever we were stationed. This time it was different, I had to learn to adapt to civilian U.S.

This was also the time when my dad started teaching me how to shoot firearms. I began shooting .22 caliber rifles in the basement range of the Army Reserve Armory. He was an expert marksman with many types of firearms, and he was a tremendous coach. He taught me to focus on the techniques of shooting, concentrate while shooting, and enjoy winning. I took to it quickly and developed the ability to tune everything else out while I was competing.

By the time I had moved from the Middle School to AC Reynolds High School I was a good shot and had joined with other shooters to form a new rifle team—we called ourselves the Mountaineers. The members of the team were all in high school, even though they lived in other parts of Asheville, went to other schools, and their families were from all walks of life. Thanks to my dad we were able to practice in the basement of the Army Reserve Armory in the winter months. When the weather got warmer, we practiced at an outdoor range not affiliated with the Army Reserve. At first, I considered the team members to be good friends, and we would share shooting techniques. However, I discovered that at least two members wouldn't share much information because their fathers had told them they needed to be the best on the team and everyone else was their competition. I was disappointed, but I didn't let it interfere with my shooting and my progress to get better. One year our team was lucky enough to go to the National Matches in Camp Perry, Ohio, which had started in 1907 and is known as "The World Series of Shooting Sports." Competitors came from throughout the U.S. and beyond including active military personnel. Camp Perry is named after Commodore Oliver Hazard Perry who defeated the British in 1813 in the Battle of Lake Erie. The camp's history during WWII included being a reception center for the new recruits and a POW camp housing both German and Italian prisoners of war. In addition to the National Matches, the camp plays a role as an Ohio Army National Guard training center.

Dad and a couple of other parents were the designated drivers in several cars for the nine hours from Asheville to Camp Perry. We would trade off riding in the cars and I hated when it was my turn to ride in the back seat of a 1960 Chevrolet Corvair. The car was small, and the back seat was cramped. It was the car that led Ralph Nader to write the book *Unsafe at Any Speed* saying it was unsafe and should be taken off the market. The car was unique, and the publicity tarnished its reputation.

The matches were several weeks long because they consisted of pistol, large bore, and small bore (.22 caliber) competition. The small bore, which is what I shot, matches were spread over a week's time. Much to the dismay of my two highly competitive teammates, I won one of the matches. The sleeping accommodations were vintage U.S. forces, where you slept in either small rooms or a large open area. The restrooms were open to the showers, sinks and toilets, and this was a terrifying experience to some civilians, to the point that a few got sick because they wouldn't use the toilet facilities frequently enough. For me, it was a normal arrangement that I had experienced before, and I thoroughly enjoyed my experience at Camp Perry. I met some excellent shooters and formed friendships. In addition, dad purchased several shooting accessories for my Remington 37 match rifle, a 7" front tube sight with clear, yellow, and green apertures, a Unertl 20 power scope, and an adjustable hook butt plate, that help me improve my skills.

Later at one competition in North Carolina, I was outside in the snow before the match started, tossing snowballs with one of my more competitive team members. He decided he would make a hard-packed snowball, and he threw it and hit me on the side of the face. At that point, I called him an asshole and went inside to wait for the match to start. He, of course, said he didn't mean to do that, but I believe he wanted to lower my focus and performance in the competition. This is where my concentration paid off. The match was close and either of us could've won. I was in position for my last shot but wasn't comfortable in my shooting position. Being out of position can lead to a bad shot. I chose not to shoot but rearrange my position instead. When shooting in competition you are shooting against the clock. All my competitors had finished shooting, including my teammate, I was the only one left on the firing line. I could see I was almost out of time, but I was determined to concentrate on this last shot. I got back in a good position, took aim, practiced correct breathing technique, and squeezed the trigger. A split second after the shot went off so did the timing buzzer. Had I shot after the buzzer sounded the shot wouldn't have counted and I would have lost the match. The shot did count, and I won the match beating my teammate and everyone else, it felt good. The skills I learned while shooting stayed with me through college and life after school. I competed on two university rifle teams, in US National matches and I won many times throughout my competition days.

The focus I learned in shooting I applied to an English assignment in school. We read *Red Badge of Courage* and was to write how we would handle the same challenge that Henry Fleming faced. I chose to put myself in Fleming's place when he had left the field of battle and was overcome with doubt. I projected myself into a military mind set, immersed in doubtful thoughts—the shame of letting my family down, the fear of failure, the fear of death. The question of my abilities and not wanting to spend the rest of my life knowing I was a coward. I ended with me determining to go into battle and accept the outcome as Fleming had done. But I wrote the paper from my point of view and given my knowledge of the war stories I had heard, my passion, and my concentration to be "in the character" made the paper a success.

Another experience of expanding my horizon was when mom made me take ballroom dancing lessons. I was embarrassed, as a teenager, to go into a studio with other people and show I couldn't dance. Week after week for six weeks, I went to the class to learn the foxtrot, waltz, mambo, and rumba to name a few. Each week I felt better about being in the class and the skill I was gaining. I survived the ordeal and learned to like dancing, although there were mistakes and stepped-on toes along the way. In fact, the ability to dance helped me through many social situations to come. This is one of those times when a parent or authority figure tells you that you need to do something, but inside you say no. When it happens, do it and you will be better off.

On the first day in high school, I was standing in line in the lunchroom when a guy approached me to ask if my name was Doug. I said no and asked why. He said his name was Joe and that a friend told him to find Doug so they could be friends. I introduced myself, and we talked and got to know one another and as it turned out he lived close to me. That chance encounter led to us becoming friends, working on school projects together, and seeing each other outside of school. One of the school projects we worked on together was a Latin class project. In which we were to do a report on the culture of the Roman Empire culture. We decided to do a report on the Roman Gladiators, and we built, with balsam wood and other materials, a gladiator school. We finished our project and made our presentation, I don't remember our grade, though I think it was good. I like to build things so when I found out that I could get old dental items from my mom, I loved it. I would get old teeth impressions and old drill burs. With that, and a small electrical motor I made a drill and played dentist. Mom also brought home some liquid mercury which was fun to roll it around, break up into pieces. Of course, at the time we didn't know that mercury could be harmful.

One of our non-school activities was when we had snow days. Joe and sometimes his younger brother Gene would walk to my house for the day. We were latchkey kids and had to fend for ourselves including lunch which was usually grilled cheese sandwiches with tomato soup. It was also the only thing we knew how to make. We found creative ways to spend our time. One of the more creative activities was bowling. I asked my mom to save the used Joy Dish Soap bottles. Her response was, "What on earth are you going to do with them?" I explained, she shook her head and said, "Okay, but you'd had better not make a mess." My friend also collected used Joy Dish Soap bottles. Soon we had a set of 10 and set up a bowling lane in my hallway. This was the first time I had a friend for any length of time because of our frequent moves. As it turned out Joe became a lifelong friend.

I was beginning to like my school and to make more friends. I remember going to a football game one Friday night and deciding to try out for the team. Well, that was a disaster, and I quickly found out that football wasn't for me. I was still spending a lot of time practicing shooting and going to matches on the weekend. I certainly didn't have time for daily football practice, Friday night games, and taking hits that would impact my shooting. So, my football days were short lived.

I consider 1963 a watershed year for me. I began to take more notice of the lunch counter sit-ins including the one at the Woolworths in Asheville, NC. Two incidents accelerated my interest in understanding the protests, and my angst over the events themselves. I was increasingly concern of where this would lead which was to the Birmingham riots in May and Governor George Wallace's attempted blocking of Black students' admission to the University of Alabama in June. I experienced a more personal incident in June while I was in downtown Asheville shopping at my favorite men's clothing store. I had left the store and turned right on Patton Avenue to walk to Pack Square where I would meet mom to drive home. I noticed a group of black students walking down Patton Avenue toward me. Normally this wouldn't have registered with me, but the year's events made me notice them. As we got closer, I also noticed they stopped their humorous interaction and put on serious faces. As we passed, there were a brushing of elbows and shoulders but nothing beyond that. This was a disappointing encounter because I believe, and had seen, people getting along even despite the difficulties. I'm also disappointed that I was a participant in the brushing, not only the recipient.

I turned sixteen in July, and it was time to get my driver's license. I had been studying and practicing but going in to take the written and driving test was nerve racking. I was even nervous about taking the eye test. All my fears were for nothing because I passed and received my license. That meant I had more freedom and could start dating in earnest, assuming I could borrow the car. I was able to borrow it a few times and started dating a beautiful young lady in my grade level. Life was good!

But life as a teenager also had its troubles. Some of my classmates were constantly getting into fights, some experienced horrible problems at home, some were drinking too much, and taking drugs. One day I got a call from a classmate who lived in my neighborhood, and she asked me to come a pick her up because she had to get out of the house and away from her abusive father. I immediately got into my car and raced to her house. She was waiting outside and jumped in when I stopped for her. She lived in a cul-de-sac, so I had to turn around and drive by her house on the way out of the neighborhood. Her father was waiting in the street as we approached. I sped up and was able to swerve the car past him and his attempt to kick the car. I took her to a local drive-in to meet a friend to stay with for a while. I felt bad and sorry for the teens who were having problems, and I was lucky that my parents were great, loving, and supportive.

CHAPTER 4

A YOUNG MAN IN PARIS

In late September of 1963, Dad received orders to go to France. I wasn't happy at all. Previous moves had felt like great adventures, but this one felt different, I was starting to have a life of my own and didn't want to give that up. I had stability in my life for the past four years, a good friend, a girl friend, shooting success, and the freedom of a driver's license. Moving meant I would have to start over, again. Plus, I couldn't get a driver's license in Europe until I was eighteen. Earlier in my life, relocation had been easier to handle because it didn't really impact me, but now it was real. I knew these moves went with Dad being in the military, so I reluctantly stepped up and did my part as well.

Dad packed his things and shipped out. Mom started the process of selling the house, arranging the movers, and shipping our car with the military authorities. She quit her job, and we separately packed our belongings to take with us on the trip to Paris. It was a hectic time, and I'm sure there were short-sighted family financial decisions made because of the time pressure. Mom accomplished the sale of the house, shipping the car and household furnishings, and all the hundreds of other things required.

On November 1963, a Tuesday, Mom and I boarded a plane at New York's Idlewild Airport, to be renamed John F. Kennedy International Airport in December 1963, bound for Paris, on a TWA 707 jet. This time our assignment was Paris, and not a small outpost. Dad had gone on earlier to check in and rent an apartment. Given our limited finances, he rented a flat in

Boulogne-Billancourt, about five miles away from Paris' city center and in a more industrial part of Paris. This neighborhood was the home of three industries, aircraft factories which started in 1906, automobile manufacturing of Renault cars and aircraft engines, and the French Film Industries' Billancourt Studios.

The flat was over a metal workshop which emitted noxious fumes and noises throughout the day. Also, small trucks would come into unload and load, the workers standing on the truck bed could look directly into our living room, which was unsettling for Mom. There were a few positives with the apartment location, it was within walking distance of small shops for bread, cheese, and bottled water. Another plus was that several times a week the entire block in front of our flat became a festive street market. These markets are considered a communal gathering and have been part of the social scene in France for centuries. There are flea markets, flower markets, books fairs, but this was one was more well-rounded and contained fresh fruits and vegetables, flowers, bread, wine, fish, meat, clothing, household items, books, and the latest gadgets. Some of the stalls offered freshly squeezed fruit juices and hot foods, a nice treat while shopping. Payment at the street market was cash only and a little price negotiation was acceptable. Even with the few positives, Mom made it clear that we needed to move. The fumes, noise and intrusion were too much of a negative. Dad immediately began to search for a much more appealing place to live.

The Friday after our arrival I enrolled in the Paris American High School located on rue Pasteur in Saint-Cloud across the Seine River, up a hill, and approximately 6 miles from the Eiffel Tower. My school, like Metz and Munich, was a U.S. Department of Defense (DoDDS) Dependent school for military and U.S. government service dependents. The school has changed and today it's the American School of Paris, a high-end private school offering an American curriculum with an international view. They're also a founding school of the International

Baccalaureate program[6]. During one of my business trips to Paris I had a chance to visit the new school. Their focus on a quality and fully rounded education was the same as I had experienced during my days at the earlier version of the school. As I walked around the campus with the headmaster, he remarked that day was a good day for me to visit because it was Parents' Day and wine was served in the school cafeteria. As we toured the arts building, I saw students painting, sculpting, and drawing not to mention the whole music wing of the campus. A better funded arts curriculum than when I was in school, although ours was great. They had converted the old gymnasium into a theater complete with orchestra pit. The students also have a well-rounded exercise program, with a lot of outdoor activities with a more international flavor such as soccer, where ours was football, basketball, and track.

That evening, November 22, 1963, after school and work, my parents and I went to the USO Club, a nonprofit organization servicing U.S. Armed Forces and their families, on the Avenue des Champs-Élysées in Paris. Being new to the city, we enjoyed talking to other military personnel and families about shopping, culture, school, and many other parts of day-to-day life in Paris. A club attendant interrupted our conversation, and we were told that there was a shooting in Dallas, Texas involving President Kennedy but, no other details were available. About an hour later we were told that he had been assassinated and all military personnel were on alert. My reaction was one of confusion and fright which slightly settled when everyone in the USO sprang into action and obviously knew what they were doing. All military personnel left to report to their assigned duty station. All the dependents went to their quarters and waited for further instructions. Dad left for his duty station which was a couple of blocks away from the USO, just off the Champs-Élysées on rue Marbeuf. It was night when Mom and I walked to the closest

---

[6] IBO.org

Metro station, Franklin D Roosevelt, to take the train to our flat. During the ride home, several French people approached us to offer their condolences. This was unexpected, but reassuring since we were in a foreign country and our President has just been assassinated. The French loved Jackie and President Kennedy, and they mourned with us.

Upon arriving at our flat we immediately tuned our radio to the BBC, per communications protocol, to wait for instructions. If instructions came, they would have been directed by the U.S. Department of State (DOS) and carried out by the U.S. DOD. This is known as a non-combatant evacuation operation (NEO) which transport, to a safe haven, those designated persons whose lives are in danger in their current foreign location. In preparation we were required to always have a bag packed for such an event and since we had just arrived in France that wasn't a problem. If instructions came for us to evacuate, we already knew to proceed to Paris Saint Lazare train station and we would be transported to our assigned embarkation Port of Le Havre. We waited in our flat until the next evening when Dad came home. His arrival meant the alert status was downgraded or cancelled, and we would not be evacuated.

Life for a recently arrived teenager in Paris under these circumstances was difficult for the next thirty days. This was the ordered period of respect for the death of President Kennedy. That meant no music in the Teen Club, PX, and Snack Bar—the places I would go to meet new people. This included curtailment of the one hour per day of Rock n' Roll music I listened to on Armed Forces Network, AFN Radio. But I survived the thirty days without music and even managed to meet new friends.

In my new school, my classmates again noticed that I wasn't wearing clothes like theirs. But this time I had the latest clothes from the United States, and they were wearing khaki pants, plaid shirts, basic dresses from the PX, or dark colored clothing purchased on the local French market. Their clothes weren't the ones they saw in the teen magazines and on record covers, which I was wearing. I received a lot of questions about my clothes and where they could get them. That sparked an idea. I got in touch with the owner of my favorite college clothing store in Asheville and asked that a catalog be sent to me in Paris. He sent me the latest catalog and I started a new business. He continued sending new catalogs so I could always offer the latest clothing to my customers. My classmates were excited to order the stylish Bass Weejuns Penny Loafers, madras cloth clothing, button down-collar shirts and socks to match, shapeless shift dresses, and many other items. I took their orders at school, sent the orders in with the money and had the merchandise back within a week. I usually got the money for the merchandise up front and occasionally upon delivery, depending upon my cash reserves. In any case, it was easy to collect because my customers really wanted the clothing. I learned that when you see an opportunity, take it. That venture helped fund my continued clothing purchase and savings.

This experience led me to begin a journey of exploration into the fashion scene in Paris as I had done previously in the US. In Paris, my wardrobe began to change to be more international rather than a US centric look. My fashion interest continued into college where I took a design class and worked in men's clothing stores. My first job out of college was with a textile company where for my training completion test, I was required to designed and make a dozen men's shirts in our factory, I also attended a course on textiles at NC State University and got hands-on experience in wool weaving in a shop back in Asheville. The Paris fashion exposure had a profound influence on the rest of my life.

Spring came and our family had moved into a new flat on rue Pasteur, a block from my school. I was continuing to make friends, increased my participation in school events and in the American community in Paris. It was clear that I needed more formal attire for many of these events. Fortunately, Hong Kong

Tailors had set up a stall at the PX. They offered tailored tuxedos including packages which included one pair of pants with a silk strip down the side seam of the legs, a black and a white jacket both with silk lapels at a reasonable price. I ordered the new tuxedos, and by the time our school's junior prom rolled around, I was ready. This was a lesson in shopping for me. A tuxedo rental for a couple of events would have cost as much or more than buying one and buying one at the PX was much less than buying one in Paris. Also, "Thank you, Mom," because my previously learned dancing skills came in handy as well.

At this point I still couldn't have a European driver's license so transportation to the prom and other events was a challenge. One of the soldiers who worked for my dad, and I considered a big brother, volunteered to be my driver and chaperone. Dad and Mom had always opened our home for the soldiers Dad worked with, and in Paris I had several that I called brothers and sisters of all races, native countries, and cultures at our home on a regular basis. To me, this extended family was a gift. I learned so much from each of them, not only as big brothers, and sisters, but about their lives and heritage. This brother's name was Vincent, and his family was originally from Sicily, but he and immediate family lived in New Jersey. He was a proper big brother and helped me navigate the evening and other challenges of my teen years in Paris.

There were other events where my tuxedos came into play. Each spring, the embassies would put on their annual Sprint Formal Parties. I wasn't on the invitee list for these events, but some classmate's families were in the diplomatic world, and I went as their guest. This was also the time when young women were present whom I hadn't yet met. These events inspired me to write. *The Young Women of Spring*. "The young women, in their summer Chanel dresses, would debut each spring at the Embassy parties. A time for excited young men, like me, to see these lovely, fresh young women for the first time. My hope was to get a chance to talk to and maybe dance with a few. I remember dancing, and the joy of being close to a beautiful lady. The feel of the elegant Chanel materials, such as soft weightless silks, the perfumed hair, and the fragrant smell of deodorant coming from their freshly shaved underarms completed the wonderful experience. At that age, it only took being there to impress me. Beyond that first encounter was something of dreams and fate."

I spent my weekends, when not with my parents, seeing Paris, going to the movies, and going to the PX to meet friends. On one trip to the PX, while checking out the latest jazz record albums, I met my soon-to-be girlfriend, and we became inseparable. We spent a lot of time together, as one would expect, and luckily, I was on good terms with her father, mother, and younger sister. Her father, a Colonel in the Army, loved to record speeches given by military leaders. I had a reel-to-reel Phillips recording device, and he would borrow it to make copies of those speeches. One time, he wanted to copy Douglas MacArthur's Farewell Speech to West Point, had been given in May 1962. He kept my recorder for several weeks and upon return it gave me a couple of new reels of recording tape and a copy of MacArthur's speech. Unfortunately, in one of our moves the tape was lost. That was one of the negatives of moving so much—things got lost.

My girlfriend and I spent many weekends in downtown Paris around the Champs-Élysées. We visited shops, museums, cafes, and the theater. When we went to the movies, museums, or performing arts events the dress code for me was nice slacks, a sport coat, white shirt and a tie and my girlfriend was a Chanel dress with appropriate shoes and bag. However, the American preppy look became acceptable attire during our outings. Any outing in the city, even just window shopping, meant that we both dressed and didn't show up in jeans and tee shirts.

We loved visiting shops like Arcades des Champs Elysees, Galeries Lafayette, Louis Vuitton, Chanel, OMEGA, Rolex,

Lancôme, Cartier, Dior, and dinnerware / glassware stores. The elegant styles, quality, vibrance, and emotion brought out by these treasures was striking. With those stimulants we began to picture what our future could be like, what we wanted to have and what we needed to do to ensure having them. For me that meant getting into and graduating college, doing my time in the military, having a successful job career (which could be in the military), and marring someone who had similar tastes and values that I had.

This Paris immersion was a great tutorial on culture and style. We always enjoyed eating croissants with orange marmalade for breakfast and a baguette, jambon, and fromage for lunch, depending upon the time we were in the city. One Saturday, I needed a haircut, so we went to the American Legion, located at 49 Rue Pierre Charron, to see my favorite barber, Alex. Alex was unique, he had a one chair operation in the American Legion building and didn't speak English. None of that mattered, we communicated, he cut my hair the way I wanted, instead of the military base barbers who would shave my head. While I was in his chair, I heard my girlfriend talking to someone, in English, in the waiting room. When Alex finished, I walked toward the waiting room and a short man came barreling by me to get into the chair. When I got to the waiting room, my girlfriend introduced me to Diana Ross. I almost feel on the floor. The man who blew by me turned out to be Barry Gordy. Ms. Ross wanted to know what it was like for American teenagers living in Paris, what music we listened to, did we miss the United States, and many other things. We continued to talk until Mr. Gordy came back from his hair cut, we said goodbye and went our separate ways. This was a big *WOW!* experience for us both.

During my senior year, I was hired to bus tables at the American Military Officers Club on Rue Marbeuf off the Champs-Élysées. After a little while I became the assistant dishwasher, which was considered a promotion. One day the salad chef didn't show up, and I became the salad chef for the day. I was sent to the kitchen minutes before the club opened and found that no prep had been done. The orders started to come in immediately for about a dozen chef salads, or at least it seemed that way. I was cutting cheese, ham, etc. from scratch and quickly became snowed under. That only lasted about an hour because I was horrible and sent back to the dishes. A good lesson about jumping in when you aren't prepared. The head dishwasher regularly gambled on the horses at the Longchamp Racecourse. One day he came into work and quit because he had won the trifecta. He was from Algeria and his winnings would give him status in his community and allow him to buy a better job in Paris. Yes, I said buy, and no, I didn't move up to head dishwasher.

One Saturday, while traveling home from the club, I had an anti-American experience in the Franklin D. Roosevelt metro station. On the platform across from mine were several boisterous youths. Once they noticed me, they started yelling obscenities and saying, "Yankee Go Home" and "We'll kick your ass." I could hear my train approaching the station, so I didn't respond to their verbal attacks, just waited for the train, boarded, and got out of there. As my train was pulling out of the station, I present them with a universal hand gesture of disrespect. The incident was a bit unnerving because I hadn't had that problem on my own in France before. I had occasionally received stares and negative looks but nothing threatening. It could've been the times in France, President De Gaulle was talking about leaving NATO in a few years and there were protests in the city from time to time by many different factions. Or it could've been youths out for a drunken Saturday evening.

The job at the club allowed me to meet interesting people and have other unique opportunities. Various celebrities came into the club—Sean Connery, Lee Marvin, and Al Viola who played with and was one of Frank Sinatra's favorite guitarists, to name a few. Mr. Viola performed one night at the club and afterwards I talked with him about music and the guitar. When I expressed my desire to learn to play the guitar, he suggested that we meet the next day, and he would help me find a guitar in the music shops. His offer was more than generous and astonished me.

The next day we met at the club and set off to find a guitar for me. Mr. Viola knew just where to go in Paris for my new instrument. In the shop he tried a few guitars and then suggested a couple to me. I immediately purchased his first suggestion at a good price. During the time we spent together, I learned about him, his music, and some of the life lessons he had learned along the way. He told me that music is hard, you must love it to do well. Guitar is a tough instrument because when you start and put in the required practice time, the tips of your fingers will hurt and bleed. That's when some people give up, but you need to keep going. My takeaway from our adventure that day was about passion, commitment, and practice.

The club held fashion shows a few times a year and I got to know the organizers, which gave me the opportunity to be a gofer during Fashion Week in Paris at some of the lesser-known events being staged. At my age, this was an eye-opening experience. Even with my limited backstage access, I was stunned by the beautiful women, dressing and undressing, and the glamor. It also helped me to continue to learn about the Paris fashion scene and my understanding of style. On a lesser redeeming note, I learned how to tell the difference between real versus augmented breasts. My breast education continued when I visited the Crazy Horse Saloon, a burlesque club, where various live performances such as comedians opened before the main act came on stage. The comedians performed their act in different languages with expressive faces, hand jesters, and impeccable timing. With that combination it didn't matter what language was spoken—you could still understand and enjoy their act.

Pop up art shows were also on the agenda at the club a few times a year offering paintings from painters throughout Europe but mainly those in France and at reasonable prices. These weren't historic works of great value, but more from artists getting their start. Once again, my family and I got to know the art dealers and had an opportunity to travel to their art gallery in Barbizon, France. There they had a large inventory of paintings, etchings, and sculptures. I bought two etchings from their inventory, one of a Paris Street and one of the Barbizon School of painter's studio, specifically Théodore Rousseau's studio, for a few francs each. I still have them, hanging in my home, and love looking at them and the memories they provide.

My senior year was a good year. By then I was a part of the fabric of this close-knit school. I was also a member of a folk group we named the Coachmen. There were four of us—two brothers from California and two of us from the southern U.S. We chose to play folk music, even though we had two California surfers in the group. I played percussion, which most of the time was bongo drums. We never got a paying gig but did play events at the school until one event where the song we sang had an unacceptable phrase in it and we were banned from then on. That didn't deter our love for music and continued playing. My shooting activities were limited in Paris. I did some practicing at the indoor range in Versailles, but no competitive matches were available. I did get a chance to shoot with the U.S. Army team on one visit to the Versailles range, my scores were impressive.

In the U.S., I was used to school fights, student discipline issues, and cliques. That wasn't the case in this school. Part of the reason was that we were a small group — there were about seventy in my senior class—and we were people with similar values and in a foreign country. But the big reason was that if we got into trouble our service-connected parents would get into trouble. I didn't want my dad being called into a superior officer's office to get a reprimand because of me. I also worked in the principal's office for my volunteer class time so getting into big trouble wasn't a part of my life.

When Senior Prom rolled around, I knew my time in Paris was getting short. I attended the prom with my only girlfriend during my time in Paris and had a terrific time. The prom was held in a restaurant located in the Bois de Boulogne, a huge park near the Seine with lakes, nature trails & botanical gardens. The restaurant had large floor to ceiling windows that allowed us to see the picturesque outside. As anticipated not long after the prom, summer came, and it was once again time to move, transfer back to the States. I had graduated and was anxious to start college. I was also fortunate that my parents were moving back to the United States as well because some of my friends weren't so lucky, as they would be separated from their families until their parents rotated back home.

My time living in Paris had to be the most defining time in my life. Even though it was only a couple of years, the impact was huge. The museums were fantastic—Rodin was a favorite—and I spent hours in the park behind the Hôtel Biron, the main building in the Sculpture Garden with vibrant green grass bordered by tall leafy trees that made it an oasis of quiet and peace. I loved sitting at the cafe in the garden watching the people and imagining their stories. One story that I wanted to capture with my camera was when I saw a French Officer, in his crisp tan uniform, sitting at a table with his smartly dress beautiful girlfriend. They were having coffee while facing each other and their hands touching. I chose not to take the shot because my shutter clicking would have broken the silence and possibly their moment. I guess that means I'm not a photojournalist. However, this museum setting gave me the canvas to create little treasures of my own with my camera.

I learned a lot about art, style, and my photographer's eye. More importantly, learning itself is a combination of study and hands on which accentuates the learning. The experience part is a critical step to help internalize what you've studied.

CHAPTER 5

UNIVERSITY & MARRIAGE

In July 1965, my family packed, shipped our household items home, and took an eight-and-a-half-hour night train from Paris Gare Du Nord station to the port of Bremerhaven, Germany. There, we boarded the USNS Alexander M. Patch, commissioned November 1944, as a troop transport—for our trip home. This was the first time traveling by ship and my first day on board was great. I met people my age and we developed a plan to find our own "teen" meeting place on board. Success came when we scouted out an aft lounge for that purpose. The lounge was out of the way, no one wanted to go down a few levels and make their way to the back of the ship, so we took it over without interference from adults. One of the teens had a battery powered record player which provided our music.

The second and third days out of port, I became seasick and didn't venture out of my room, except to go to the restroom and eat a little food. My fourth day I was back having fun in the "Teen Club." Mom, however, was seasick the whole trip and she could only eat saltine crackers and drink water. Dad didn't get seasick and was fine until we were one day out of New York, when he received a radio gram that his mom had passed away. After receiving the news, Dad kept to himself the last bit of the trip. He was anxious to get off the ship to attend her funeral, in West Virginia, scheduled for the day after we docked. We had shipped two cars home earlier, so dad took the 1964 TR4, a Triumph sports car, and left first for his hometown. Mom and I followed in the 1963 Pontiac Tempest. Dad made it in time for the funeral by, I suspect, driving fast. Mom and I arrived a day later. It was a sad time but a time of good memories of my grandmother Kirk, Sunday dinners, her handmade quilts, and sweets. She was also a tough lady, having had to survive in a small hill town in West Virginia with six kids and a husband who creatively scraped out a living. Mom and I stayed with her mother, in a neighboring town because of the limited sleeping quarters at Dad's mother's house. Staying with grandmother Wiles-Parsley was familiar and comforting. Her house was on two acres, one of which was a garden. She kept chickens and when we had chicken for dinner, she would go out back, grab a chicken, and ring its neck to kill it, clean, and cook it. It was a gruesome sight to see the chicken running around without its head, but that was the way it was done. We slept on feather beds that we would sink into a deep crevice, greatly restricting my movement at night. Her lighting and cooking energy source was from natural gas because the family owned a couple of shares in a natural gas company, which was plentiful in that part of the country.

A couple of days later, we said goodbye to Dad's brothers and sister and left for Fort McPherson in Atlanta, dad's next duty assignment. Upon arrival on base, dad was told his unit had shipped out to Viet Nam the week before, and the Army was trying to decide to either ship him out or find another assignment for him. We didn't want him to be shipped out since we just got back from Europe and would rather, he be given an assignment at Fort McPherson. It took the Army most of the day, while we waited outside in the hot sun in our car, to make the decision that he would remain there. After Dad finished checking in on base, we drove to Asheville, N.C. where my parents decided that they would make their permanent home. Mom would stay there regardless of where dad's assignment might take him, because he only had a couple of years left before his retirement. Mom and Dad purchased a house in our old neighborhood in Oteen, and our belongings were sent to the new house. Dad would come home to Asheville on weekends but worked in Atlanta during the week.

With our family life settled, I turned my attention to college. I didn't know much about the U.S. universities, so I took my aunt's advice and applied to the Tennessee Technological University in Cookeville, where my cousin Don was enrolled in electrical engineering. Since I had been in transit, I hadn't received an acceptance or rejection letter from the school. When we had settled into our new home in Asheville, in August of 1965, I called the university admissions office to ask if I had been accepted. I was told that they were still processing admissions and were trying to finish by fall registration, and that I should show up during registration in September and find out. For some reason, I wasn't concerned or anxious about getting admitted, I assumed it would happen. I was excited about going to college but not stressed out.

When it was time for fall semester to start, I packed up and headed off to Tennessee Technological University. in Cookeville, a small town located in the Highland Rim of the Cumberland Plateau between Nashville and Knoxville, currently three miles off I-40 which is the main east-west highway across Tennessee. As I arrived in the center of Cookeville, I saw a large arrow painted black with a gold rim and lettering hanging over an intersection pointing right. The sign read "Tenn Tech 8 Blocks." The campus itself was about six by six blocks in size. The buildings were between one and three stories high, including the dormitories.

I parked my car and found the admissions office. To my dismay, they didn't have any record of my application, but said "Well you are here now so let's get you registered." I spent the day filling out an application, forms for transcripts, and what seemed like a never-ending stack of paperwork. It took all day to sort things out and gain admission. Once that was done, I was assigned a dormitory and proceeded to check in with the dorm resident advisor who assigned me my specific room. My roommate wasn't in, so I unloaded my car and made the only unmade bed in the room. During this process my roommate came in from dinner and we started to get to know one another. I hadn't eaten since breakfast, I didn't receive a cafeteria card at the admissions office, that I would have to get that the next day at registration. I asked him where to find food and he suggested a small diner just off campus about two blocks away. I walked to the diner, which would become a place where I would eat frequently. I remember having a hamburger and fries. The hamburger was a double decker something like the Big Mac of today. While eating, I reflected on the fact that I should've done more research on universities and followed up with Tennessee Technical University about my admission rather than just assume things were set.

The next morning, I went to the gym where class selection and schedule was taking place. I was given a computer printout of my classes and schedule, no choices because all freshmen had to take the same classes, the only variance was the specific days and times. The only choice I was given was whether to enroll in the Army ROTC program or not and I enrolled. I also wanted to find out where to join the rifle team and was directed to the armory on campus. There I found the Army Sergeant, the military advisor, and signed up for the team.

My reason for going to college was twofold. First, I wanted to graduate with a degree in business, and second, I wanted to make the military my career by completing advanced ROTC and be commissioned in the Army as a Second Lieutenant. After that, I would serve my compulsory time, during which I would evaluate my decision to make the military my career.

My daily routine was simple: go to class, go to the armory to practice shooting, and an occasional trip with the rifle team. One of the highlights of the week was watching the TV series Star Trek in the resident advisor's room, the only TV allowed in the dorm. One evening, after ROTC drill several of us got back to the dorm just before the show started. We quickly got out of our military fatigues and ran to watch the show, wearing only our tidy whities. The resident advisor shook his head and laughed as did everyone else, as they saw that I had my underwear on inside out.

I enjoyed going to the indoor rifle range at the armory to practice my shooting for several hours at a time. The rifle team members were friendly, and it was a familiar setting which helped me comfortable with college life. The team had a history of many wins, many national titles, and all-American athletes. This team was no different, a team of excellent shooters consisting of both women and men, I had to do my best to measure up. Which I did by helping the team win matches and some individual match wins. We received financial subsidies from the military and a little from the university. The financial support from the Army allowed us to buy some of the best rifles at the time, such as Winchester 52, Remington 40x, and Walther KKM Free Rifles, equipped with iron sights and without scopes. I was assigned the Winchester 52. We had a regular schedule of matches against other universities, and for some of them, we traveled to those schools. We would pack and climb into our school vans, travel to the match, shoot, and travel home. During the few trips that were longer, we stayed overnight in inexpensive motels, four to a room. Any meals were picked up by the Army Advisor. The university considered us a club sport, but eligible to get a school letter with our club insignia on the letter, which I received. I loved every minute of the practice, the trips, the competing, and the camaraderie.

After joining the rifle team, I was asked to join the Pershing Rifles drill team. As a member of the Pershing Rifles drill team, I had to go through initiation. That consisted of shaving my head, wearing green cotton fatigues, carrying a wooden hand-made saber, and a pail, painted blue and white with the letters PR on the side, filled with water and a single goldfish. Of course, anytime you saw an upper classman who was a Pershing Rifles member, you got grief, and if your goldfish was dead, you had to eat it then and there. So, my fellow inductees and I had a backup pail loaded with goldfish in case ours died. The initiation lasted a week, and it wasn't that bad. Having been around the military, I was familiar with the process, the mandatory pushups and having to recite the Pershing Rifles creed, usually in group formation in the middle of the quad area where many students would gather to watch the spectacle or at the discretion of a higher-ranking member, any time, any place. We were also required to double time[7] everywhere we went on campus. Being a part of the rifle team and the Pershing Rifles allowed me to shoot in competition for the Pershing Rifles where I won both regional and national medals.

I was always looking for ways to make money and I quickly discovered that most freshmen ROTC students had no clue on how to shine their shoes, clean their brass, or iron their shirts with the correct creases. I saw an opportunity to have another small business, so I started doing those things for them and charging for my work. Several months later I discovered that the town was dry, meaning no alcohol was permitted. Another opportunity, as I occasionally traveled home, I would buy a few pints of alcohol in our state-run ABC stores in Asheville and bring them back for sale. But that business didn't last long because the local police started putting up roadblocks on Sunday afternoon and evening to catch anyone hauling alcohol into the town or campus. Luckily, I was never stopped.

Our family life during my time at Tennessee Tech was normal. What I mean by normal is unsettled for most. Mom got a job at the VA Hospital near our house in Asheville and I settled into college. It was different for Dad because his time at Ft McPherson only lasted for a couple of months. The Dominican Republic was embroiled in a civil war from mid to late 1965. Lyndon B. Johnson, our U.S. President, was convinced that the

---

[7] Normal military pace is 120 steps per minute, double time is 180 steps per minute.

Loyalist forces who were pro-America would be defeated, and that a second Cuba would be created. President Johnson ordered U.S. forces to enter Dominican Republic. Dad was deployed, as part of a "peacekeeping force", where he would stay for six months. When Christmas came Dad wanted us to have presents even though he couldn't be with us. Mom went out and bought presents and she and I wrapped them. Around midnight on Christmas Eve, I was sleeping when I heard a noise outside and saw car headlights. Mom and I got up to answer the door when the bell rang, which gave us an uneasy feeling since my father was deployed in a troubled area of the world. Mom opened the door, and it was Dad. He was in his military fatigues[8] carrying a rucksack[9] and a holstered .45 caliber sidearm. He had arranged to get a military aircraft hop and civilian transport from Dominican Republic to Asheville. But he had less than twenty-four hours to stay, and then he had to catch the return military aircraft back to the Dominican Republic.

The day after his arrival, he and mom had a serious talk just before he had to leave. After Dad left, mom approached me about our Christmas presents. She asked if I would be okay not to keep them that year but return them because she and Dad needed to save the money. I immediately agreed because I wanted to do what was best for our family and frankly, spending a few hours with both mom and dad at Christmas was present enough. I learned later that dad had written us a note apologizing for not providing enough money for us to have presents and he felt his visit had upset our Christmas. I became emotional when I read it, as he always did everything to provide for us and his short visit made a great Christmas.

After Dominican Republic, he came back to the States and returned to Ft McPherson. That stint lasted for a few months, when

---

[8] Called combat uniform, field uniform, battledress or military fatigues.

[9] A gab carried by a strap on your back or shoulder.

he was reassigned to Seoul, Korea. His job there was to oversee the storage and use of classified documents primarily about North Korea and China. When he took over the job, he had to sign for all the documents in the vault, which meant that if any document went missing it was his hide that got tanned. If someone wanted to see a document, they had to sign for it and dad would have to approve it, and the document couldn't leave the premises. When it was time for dad to come back to the United States he had to account for and sign out all the documents. On his last night in Seoul, he was escorted to dinner and drinks by two military security personnel. They also escorted him to his plane and stayed in the terminal until the plane had taken off. That was his last duty assignment. As he came back his retirement and transfer to Army Reserve status was processed at Fort Lewis, outside of Tacoma, Washington. He had finished his twenty plus years of military service and was going home to Asheville and my mom.

Meanwhile, I was still at Tennessee Tech University but growing more unhappy with my university selection. The university was small, comfortable, and okay but there were only a few students who were majoring in business and even fewer female students on campus. My cousin was finishing his senior year in engineering, so I paid him a visit one evening to share my concerns. When I completed my griping about the few business students and fewer ladies at the school, his answer was, "of course, this is a technical school" "If you want a good business school and more social life you should transfer to the University of Tennessee." I took his advice and applied to the University of Tennessee in Knoxville. I filled out the forms to apply for a transfer, even though my friends told me it was hopeless. Several of them had applied for a transfer, more than once, and hadn't been accepted.

After a couple of weeks, I began to look for an acceptance or rejection letter in my mailbox. That became a daily activity until one day I received my acceptance letter from the University of

Tennessee in Knoxville. My start date was set for January 1967. My Tennessee Tech friends were astonished and upset that I was accepted for transfer, and they hadn't been. Some of them had been trying for over two years. I didn't know why I had been accepted but was happy to be moving on at the beginning of the next school year. It was my last day at As Tennessee Tech and I packed my car to leave after my last exam, a friend helping me pack and when loading my car saw a few grains of sand on my car's gas cap. Dad still was in Seoul, Korea so I, was driving the Triumph TR4 which had a gas cap between the trunk and back glass of the car, meaning it was on top of the trunk area. I asked my friend what he thought it was and his reply was it could be nothing or it could be that someone put sand in my gas tank. Either way he recommended that I get it checkout. I asked for his advice on checking it out. He said I had to drain the gas out of the tank to see if there was any sand. If not, then okay but if so, it would require cleaning. At that point I was upset, confused and I needed to go to my last exam. Luckily, he said he had worked on cars all his life and would check it out. By the time I got back from my exam he had finished the work and said there wasn't sand in the gas tank. Apparently, it had been a practical joke. I thanked him, offered to pay which he refused, and jumped in my car for my final trip from Cookeville to my home in Asheville, NC.

When school started in January, I packed my TR4 and drove to Knoxville. The roads to Knoxville were two lane US Highways going through mountains so great care needed to be taken in winter months. However, my favorite route was over the Great Smokey Mountains National Park which contained high mountains with small and winding roads, and in winter months it was often closed because it was too dangerous or completely impassable.

I was excited when I arrived in Knoxville for the first time. The city was considerably larger, one hundred eighty-seven thousand population versus fourteen thousand in Cookeville. Of course, nowhere near the over seven million people[10] in Paris, France. My drive in was from the east, and to my left as I came across the Henley Street Bridge was Neyland Stadium, the football stadium with a capacity of sixty-four thousand, jumped out at me. After crossing the bridge, I turned left on Cumberland Avenue, nicknamed the "Strip," which took me to the campus. The strip was a place that had restaurants, shops, bookstores, bars, and clubs, a perfect hangout and place for students to spend their money. It was obvious that I was in the University of Tennessee territory because I saw a sea of orange and white, the school colors, and it was significantly larger than the six square blocks of Tennessee Tech. At a traffic light I asked for and got directions to Hess Hall, my dormitory. Upon arrival I had to ride around a while to find a parking spot because of the thousands of students checking in, but I did and checked into Hess Hall, a men's only dormitory[11]. After getting my room assignment, I unloaded my car and settled into my new home for the next few years. Throughout the year the dormitory had ongoing activities to keep the residents occupied. I remember we had Otis Redding singing his new song "Dock of the Bay," in our lobby. addition, the school had concerts, like James Brown, and various speakers to entertain and expand our minds.

I was two days early so I could hopefully see my faculty advisor before the official registration started. My next step was to schedule a meeting and luckily, I got an appointment the next day. When I went to the advisor's office in the Glocker business building for my meeting, the advisor started by going over my transcript so he could advise me on what courses to take. After reviewing my file, he put it down and looked up with a quizzical expression. "Since you've been getting A grades in engineering and physics, why did you transfer to this school, when Tennessee Tech would offer you more?"

---

[10] Paris 1965 population 7.855 million, macrotrends.net

[11] It wasn't until my senior year that the university instituted coed dorms.

My reply was that my major was in business and not engineering. He looked at the transcript again, then looked back at me. He started to say, "Then why…" but stopped and started to laugh. I then knew why I was admitted so quickly, and others weren't, and I started to laugh. Apparently, the registrar's office at Tennessee Tech had pulled the transcript of someone who made straight A grades in engineering and physics and sent it as mine. I don't know if that person's name was John Kirk or not. But I swear I had nothing to do with the transcript mix-up. After the advisor and I had a good laugh, he said, "Well you are here now so let's get you started on your business major," A familiar phrase I had heard at Tennessee Tech and seemed to define my college experience. I felt extremely relieved that I could stay, otherwise I wouldn't have been enrolled in any university.

The next day I went to the course enrollment hall to see what I could get in the way of classes. Since I hadn't had a chance to pre-register, I had to run to table after table to see if I could still get into some of the courses I needed. At the end of the day, I had done well, which included signing up for ROTC. There were tables set up in the hall to attract students to sign up for their choice of over fifty different clubs. I didn't sign up for any because I knew my plate was full and I wanted to know more about the various clubs before signing up.

Now on to the bookstores to buy books. Book buying here was much better because I had several bookstore choices. I started with the on-campus store and found most of what I needed, but I ran to the off-campus stores to purchase the remaining books. Back at my dorm room I pulled out my class schedule and a campus map to see where I had to be the next morning at 8 a.m. Yes, I had to take a dreaded 8 a.m. class. With that done, my roommate and I ventured out to find dinner.

My first day of classes started with me hiking from my dorm, up many hills and finally the administration area infamously called the Hill, that hike up the final hill alone seemed like hundreds of steps. It looked like I would certainly get my exercise over the next few years. On that first day of classes, I had breaks in my schedule and used the time to find the rifle range and join the rifle team. After meeting the military advisor, I was asked to come back two days later to meet the team and show what I could do. I had packed my shooting gear, except my rifle, and would have to use one of the issued rifles to demonstrate my abilities. While at the range, I asked about the Pershing Rifles but was told that the organization didn't have a chapter at UT. Two days later, I showed up at the range, met the rest of the male and female team members and I was handed an Anschutz Match 54 Model 1413 rifle and ammo to demonstrate my skills. I shot all four positions, prone, sitting, kneeling, and standing. After I had finished, my scores were good, and I was accepted by the team as a member.

While I was at Tennessee Technological University, I had won several medals for regional and national rifle matches and for the drill team. I was allowed to wear the corresponding ribbons on my ROTC uniform as well as the shoulder cords, fourragère[12], for the rifle team and Pershing Rifles. When I got to University of Tennessee, I noticed most of the ROTC uniforms were plain, and to the contrary, mine stood out. The joke was that whenever the Army Colonel, our ROTC advisor, saw me he would jokingly address me as "General." But at least I got noticed.

I enjoyed being on the rifle team, which was sponsored by the ROTC program with an Army Sergeant as our coach. The University of Tennessee also considered it a club sport unlike football, baseball, and basketball, and we could be awarded letters and could wear university sweaters and the like. As before, our inter-university shooting matches were usually conducted on weekends and followed a planned schedule for the year. We would

---

[12] The fourragère is a military award and distinguishing military units in the form of a braided cord.

travel, mainly in the southeast, to compete or other university teams would visit us in Knoxville. Unlike Tennessee Tech I had on a few occasions, the chance to see friends at other schools. On one such trip to N.C. State University, I met up with a friend from my Asheville days. I asked and got permission to stay the rest of the weekend with him and not travel home with the rifle team. He had an off-campus apartment, and I had a great weekend hanging out with him and his friends. Monday morning, we loaded into his 1959 Corvette for the trip back to Knoxville. Instead of going straight back, we made several stops along the way to visit other friends from my Asheville days who were attending schools in Durham, Winston-Salem, and Greensboro. It was winter and his 1959 Corvette's heater wasn't working well, and the rag top had several holes that let in cold air, but it was a grand adventure. Traveling on weekends meant that I didn't always get to participate in on-campus events such as football games and it cut down on my visits home to Asheville, but I still felt that being on the rifle team was worth the time, effort, and travel.

One of the reasons I moved to this school was for a larger female population. When it came to the college women, they were a disappointment. I found that they were cliquish and aloof, not close to the caliber of women I encountered in Europe. I tried dating but none of my dates seem to go past the first date or two. It was probably me because I wasn't in sync with their likes, dislikes, and priorities, or how to spend our time. I understood they wanted to take part in every campus activity they could, and I guess there were two main deal breakers: first, they wanted to go to every football game with a date, and I was out of town because of the rifle team for many of the games, and second, they wanted to date fraternity guys, which I wasn't. I had chosen to be an independent because I didn't see the benefit of devoting one hundred percent of my time to the fraternity when I had other priorities. And there could've been a third reason—I could've been too snobbish and had different expectations after living in and graduating from high school in Europe.

In the spring of 1967, I got a shock: my draft notice came. My legal residency was McMinnville, Tennessee and while I had transferred schools, the paperwork of that transfer hadn't made it to the through the system. So, the Draft Board thought I had quit school, and therefore couldn't have student deferment status. I was in my second year of ROTC, so I went to the Army Colonel Advisor to find out how my being in ROTC impacted the draft notice. He said, "Well, you are about to become a junior in school, which means you can go advanced ROTC. Signing the paperwork to go advanced means you are in the Army with all the associated commitments. Being in the Army would negate any draft induction." He offered and I immediately signed the paperwork. With that done, I could continue my education and then go into the Army, which was my goal anyway.

But I still had to board a Greyhound bus in Knoxville for a trip to Nashville for my draft screening process. After checking in at the draft center, I was told to strip down to my underwear bottoms and shoes, get in line with my draft paperwork. I went through several stations devoted to my physical condition. Everything from eyesight to "turn your head and cough". At one of the stations, I was asked if I ever had any medical problems. I said, "No, except when I was in Munich, Germany I was treated for a stomach problem by the military doctors." I was afraid not to tell them since my records might be checked. The doctor then asked the nature of the stomach problem. "Stomach pains that lasted for a few days and not come back for a few months. The military doctors gave me a white chalky liquid to drink when I got the pains," I explained. I further said that when I got back to the U.S. a local doctor in Asheville had examined me and said I had a duodenal ulcer. I presented my civilian medical records to the draft doctors, and I was immediately rerouted to an exam room where I was poked around my abdomen. After that exam I was told to get my clothes on and wait in the lobby. I never had a chance to present my advanced ROTC status. After several of us guys assembled in the lobby we were taken to a larger room where we were told our draft status was now 1Y, temporary deferment to being drafted. They also said that some of us might be getting a 4F rating, which changed the temporary to permanent status. I eventually received the 4F rating.

I still don't believe I had the ulcer; I think my stomach issues were just from stress and nerves. I also think the local civilian doctor was just trying to help keep me out of potentially being drafted. Any way you look at it, my hoped-for military career was over. The trip on the bus back to Knoxville was a sad one. My plans and dreams were dashed, and I had to carry the label of someone not fit for military service. I also dreaded facing the Colonel, but the next morning after my return, I went to him and told him what happened. He said, "No problem. Sorry to hear you won't be joining advanced ROTC or going in the Army." He then reached in a desk drawer, pulled out my paperwork, tore it up, and deposited it in the trash can. With my life plans derailed, it took a while to shake my feeling of being rudderless and to re-prioritize my future. The process meant that I had to go through the five stages of grief: denial, anger, bargaining, depression, and finally acceptance.

I continued to go home when my schedule permitted. Unfortunately, on one trip home, the Smokey Mountain National Park route was open, but caution was warned, I took the route anyway. I had left school late, and it would be after dark when I arrived in Asheville. I had made it over the mountains and was on my descent, so I picked up speed. As I came around a curve, hit black ice and started to spin. Luckily, I crashed to my right mountain side instead of my left, the gorge side. I got out, still had dry pants, checked the damage, and decided to continue driving home slowly. As I pulled into my house, Dad came out immediately because he knew something was wrong. It took almost a year to get the car fixed since it was a British sports car, and no one around Asheville knew how to work on it.

I admit that my grades were bad, which led to a university-dictated sitting out for a quarter in the spring of 1968. I packed up and went home but I didn't sit around. As my dad strongly suggested, I got a job. I found a job working in retail men's clothing, something I knew a lot about. However, this job wasn't permanent, I was determined to reapply at the university as soon as my waiting period was over. I enjoyed helping customers with their clothing needs and the accolades from management for my strong sales numbers. But I also reapplied for admission to the University of Tennessee, which was granted, and I went back to school for the summer quarter of 1968. From that point on, my grades continued to improve and there were no more interruptions in my education. A good lesson that reinforced the concept of hard work is needed to be successful.

A friend had suggested many times that I come home, and he could arrange dates with nursing students at Memorial Mission Hospital. He already had his eye on one of the students and suggested we go on a double date with one of her classmates. I agreed and when date night came, we picked them up at their dormitory and went to a play at a local theater. When we found our seats, with the women seated between us guys. My date and I seemed to be getting along, but I kept looking at and becoming more intrigued by my friend's date, whose nick name was Sam. I began to talk to her more than my date. First, she was beautiful with long dark hair, big round eyes, long eye lashes, land light olive skin. She came across as the opposite of the women at school who were cliquish, aloof, loud, and insincere. She was shy and a nice person. With that combination I had to see her again. After we dropped off the women, my friend and I agreed to pursue each other's dates in the future. As you can imagine, the women were skeptical to say the least. But over time I began dating Sam regularly. Our relationship developed and we began juggling schedules for me coming home or Sam visiting me in Knoxville. She graduated before me and moved home to live with her parents in Boiling Springs, North Carolina and work locally as a nurse.

My visits home became less since I was visiting her at her parents. I was happy to be dating this beautiful, sincere, and nice person because she was the woman I had hoped to find.

On one of my visits home Dad pulled me aside to talk about my future. The conversation was straight forward, "Son you have three things to accomplish over the next couple of years. First, graduate, the second thing is to get a job when you graduate, and the third is get married." He didn't mention going into the military because that option had been taken off the table. Had that option not been taken away he would have said, graduate, go into the military, and get married at some point in the future. Marrying after spending time in the military is better because trying to do both is hard. I knew that I would graduate soon and getting a job would be something to work on, and I would ask Sam to marry me around that time, which I did by proposing in the parking lot at Fort McPherson Post Exchange in Atlanta. The reason we were there was my parents had access to the base PX so an engagement ring could be purchased at a much lower price than from a normal civilian retailer. So, in the back seat of their car, I proposed, and she said yes. We began planning our wedding for June of 1969. The wedding was held at Sam's hometown church in Boiling Springs. Afterwards we left to spend a weekend honeymoon in Gatlinburg, Tennessee.

After the brief honeymoon, we packed our belongings and immediately went back to the university and moved into the married student housing. The housing was a newly completed twenty-one-story high rise, nick named the Tide Box because of its shape, just off campus. Our apartment was small, with one bedroom, one bath, a living area, and a small kitchen area.

Our life there was simple, Sam worked at a local hospital, on the evening shift, and I attended classes during the day. I picked up part-time work during school breaks and holidays as a delivery van driver for an office supply store. We were both focused on my graduating, getting a job, and starting our life outside of school. I also noticed that my grades significantly improved now that I was married and had obligations.

A memorable event happened just after moving in. On July 20, 1969, I was in our apartment, and Sam was working second shift. I was watching the Moon landing on TV but wanted to quickly take the trash out. I hurriedly gathered the trash and went out the door to the garbage chute. When I came back to my door it was locked, I had forgotten to take a key in my rush to take the garbage out and get back to the Moon landing. Luckily, the building superintendent was available to let me in the apartment, but I almost missed the landing. Sam missed the actual landings full coverage because of her work but saw the replays. It was a spectacular sight and a great achievement.

As I finished my last months in college, I was excited to be graduating with a degree in business and looking forward to putting into practice what I had learned. I didn't fully realize that this was just the beginning of my learning about business and success—in other words, learning what the schools and teachers hadn't taught me about being successful.

During that time, I saw protests began springing up about many different topics. At the end of 1969, our beloved university president Andy Holt was retiring, and a new president needed to be named. During Christmas break, the trustees met and named Ed Boiling president. When the students and faculty came back on campus, they were upset by the appointment, which led to protests outside of the administration building in January 1970. That protest led to arrests and a charge of felony, later reduced to lesser charges. There were discussions with the administration, students, and faculty but nothing changed, and Ed Boiling remained president. After my graduation, there were Vietnam war protests. Kent State, in May 1970, was one of those protests that turned deadly when several students were shot, killing four and wounding nine. That lead to a protest on our campus on later that month.

II

LEARNING THE BUSINESS GAME

CHAPTER 6

GREAT MENTORS

When I graduated on March 1970, the job market was poor, and I didn't secure a job prior to graduating. I did sign up to interview with the few companies who came to campus to recruit but nothing came of that effort. Sam and I were amenable to relocating wherever a job would take us but for the job search we started by targeting the locations near where we had relatives; at least we'd have food and a place to stay during my job search. We had two options, Boiling Springs, North Carolina, where her parents lived or Asheville, North Carolina, where my parents lived. We chose Boiling Springs because it was closer to Charlotte, North Carolina with more companies and hopefully better job options. We settled into our temporary housing, and I began my job search. I updated my resume with my graduation details and new contact information, and added content that companies may want from what I learned interviewing.

Next, I gathered up phone books, checked the Sunday newspapers, and researched recruiting firms for Charlotte and Atlanta. With that I started making phone calls, submitted letters, and resumes. I then did follow up phone calls to secure phone interviews and few face-to-face interviews.

It took several weeks of this full-time job search with first step rejections, second-third-forth step rejections until I landed a position as the Human Resources and Payroll Manager for a textile plant in Kings Mountain close to Boiling Springs. The plant was part of Oxford Industries, an Atlanta, Georgia-based clothing company. The current manager was promoted to Human

Resources Area Manager and needed to back-fill his position. The opportunity was perfect for me, it was in my career path and close enough to both of our parents.

The Kings Mountain plant made men's Ban-Lon[13] type knit shirts, they were made with synthetic yarn and stylish at the time. The production went from melting small pellets into thread, then knitting into fabric, cutting the patterns, sewing into garments, and dyeing the finished clothing. Kings Mountain was originally called White Plains and was changed to Kings Mountain when incorporated in October 1874. The change was made due to its closeness to the historic 1780 Battle of Kings Mountain site in York County South Carolina. The significance of the battle and Battle was, "the turning point of the American Revolution" proclaimed Thomas Jefferson.

At first, I commuted twenty-one miles from Boiling Springs to Kings Mountain while looking for a house. Thanks to the help of people in the plant Sam and I were able to find a house to rent within a couple of weeks. The house was nice, two bedrooms, a single bath, large living room and dining room combined, a large screened in porch and big back yard. It sat elevated at the end of a street overlooking ten duplex rentals, five on each side of the street. It was a close community because at the end of the day and on weekends people were out in the street talking to neighbors and playing with their kids. With a new job and a house to live in, we were now off and running in our new life together.

I began my career journey with great enthusiasm. My staff consisted of two payroll clerks, one was in charge, and the other was her assistant, and a receptionist. I was the only one handling Human Resources. The senior payroll clerk had been in the

---

[13] Ban-Lon is a trademarked, multi-strand, continuous-filament synthetic yarn used in the retail clothing industry.

business for several years and had seen young managers straight out of college come and go. She ran her payroll office, and everyone needed to know and accept that. I was fine with the arrangement because I had much to learn and of course being fresh out of college I was subject to some hazing, which I expected, and didn't let it bother me. The plant manager was a guy who had been in the textile business for a long time, with a lot of knowledge and experience. He was also a good guy who would sometimes drink adult beverages with his management staff, after hours, a unique experience for me.

The plant was in a small town with several other textile plants. The population of Kings Mountain was 21,914 in 1970, and that meant all the employers were competing for the small talent pool. Our plant had 600 employees with a high turnover, which required me, as the Human Resources Manager, to constantly be recruiting new employees. The plant itself was new, which made it a better place to work than some of the older mills, as they were called, in the area.

Each Monday morning, one of my tasks—which I didn't like to do—was to find out who didn't show up for work, call the local police to see if they were in jail, and if so get them out. If not in jail, I would seek help from other employees in the plant to find out why the person wasn't at work. Sometimes that meant going to the missing person's home, something that wouldn't be a good idea today, to see if they were there. In every case, my job on Mondays was to get people to work, always a challenging task.

Another unpleasant task was terminating a poor performing employee. I would be the one to tell the employees they were fired and to leave the premises. I remember one woman who was constantly absent from work, even after warnings and write ups. On one of the few days, she came to work, I brought her into the office and terminated her employment. The next day, after she was fired, her husband called me to ask why. He started the call by saying "I'm coming to your office and whip your ass." I told him that I couldn't tell him why his wife was fired, and "I'm in my office every day from 7:00 AM until 6:00 PM if you want to come by." He did come into the office at 5:00 PM that day, he wasn't as aggressive in person as on the phone, but he continued to ask the same question about why his wife had been fired. "You should ask her if she was at work every day she was scheduled or not," I said. His face turned pale and there was silence for at least 15 seconds, then he said, "Oh, I'll handle this sorry to bother you." That was the last I heard of him or his wife.

I kept remembering how my father approached any task with a commitment to "get the job done." My father's military background and results driven approach made a lasting impression, something I keep with me to this day.

One day, I had to do time and motion studies in our sewing department. Because the department's productivity wasn't at the level expected and we needed to know what was wrong. I guess I was selected because I knew how to do the studies, and the department supervisor wasn't getting the job done. Also, worker's pay depended upon the number of pieces they turned out during their shift, and we wanted to make sure that was calculated properly. I prepared my data capturing sheets with great zeal, got my stopwatch, and off I went. As I charged in and started performing the task, I noticed that the workers weren't friendly. Of course, I paid no attention, but was quickly called away by the plant manager—my boss—and admonished for causing chaos in the department. I was devastated because I had messed up an important assignment.

As time passed and with reflection on the incident, I learned a valuable lesson in communication. In this situation, what was needed was to make sure the department manager communicated to the employees what was going to happen and the reasons why in advance. Upon arrival in the department, I needed the manager to pull everyone together, introduce me, and again, explain what was going to happen and why. As I sat with the employees, I needed to be respectful of their time and reiterate what I was going to do and ask for their help in doing my assignment. I also should've asked the employees if they knew of anything that would help them do their job better.

That was a humbling experience and what I learned I added to my portfolio. My enthusiasm wasn't dampened, and I was still full of myself. Yet I had many more lessons to learn. Even though I was enthusiastic and driven, this experience was my first career lesson in the fine art of diplomacy and the softer side of business. That was when I added to my father's "get the job done" approach the phrase "with finesse."

Later in my employment with the company, I was transferred to the Atlanta Corporate office to take the position of Merchandising Manager for the JC Penny dress shirt line. Sam and I moved to Marietta, GA, a suburb of Atlanta and rented a townhouse. Sam got in touch with a nursing school friend living in Marietta who recommended her to Northside Hospital, where she was hired as a nurse. We both had commutes of about thirty minutes to and from work. One of the interesting things about where we lived was a couple of miles away from the end of the runway at Dobbins Air Force Base and Lockheed manufacturing plant. Air Force planes and the new planes being tested would fly over our townhouse when approaching the runway. At that time Lockheed was building and testing the C5 Galaxy aircraft. The aircraft was large at over two hundred forty-seven feet. long, over two football fields and a height of sixty-five feet. When the C5 flew over us it was so big it seemed like it wasn't moving, and the sky darkened.

Working in the corporate office was my first taste of corporate politics. It took some time to learn who had the power and who didn't because it's complicated and you can't always tell by some's title. Sometimes a person may have power and not be in a power position, but they're an influencer. With this company, I learned the power structure by asking people whom they thought had the power, not always the most accurate source of information, by listening and observing actions that reveal power directly or through influence. But it was much later in my career life that I received training on how to accurately determine the corporate power structure.

My first assignment was to go to our manufacturing plant in Vidalia, Georgia to attend an orientation program for my new position in merchandising. Vidalia was 172 miles from Atlanta and a three-hour drive, which I completed in my bright yellow VW Bug. Upon arrival, I went to the plant to meet the plant manager and my coach for my visit. The schedule for the week was well laid out, and it would culminate with me making a dozen shirts on my own. During the week I learned about fabrics, patterns, and sewing. I began my learning about fabrics with polyester, the fabric widely used at the time, and a fabric I don't like for shirts, but I prefer 100% pima cotton for dress shirts. The JC Penny shirt orders were both polyester and cotton, I needed to learn all the fabrics. At the end of my first day, I checked into my motel for the week which was a throwback from fifteen to twenty years before. It was on a single level with twenty individual rooms where the doors open directly onto the gravel car park. If you wanted ice, there was an ice maker outside at the end of the building. The rooms were small, clean, simple, but outdated.

The rest of the week I learned about shirt patterns and how to lay them out for plain, striped, and checked shirts. My sewing education included learning to sew using a standard single needle, a double needle and bar-tack[14] machines. By the end of the week, I was ready to make my dozen shirts. I selected my fabrics, cut the

---

[14] Bar-tack - stitches used to reinforce areas of a garment subject to stress and wear

shirts with the pattern I wanted, and started sewing. That was Thursday afternoon and by the end of the day I had finished one shirt. The ladies working in the sewing area took pity on me and decided I needed help. "It's time for you to go to your motel and we'll finish your shirts," they said. And Friday morning when I came in my shirts were finished. Of course, the plant manager and my coach knew what had happened and they just laughed. They gave me a passing grade on my orientation, and I suspect other trainees received the same treatment. I did learn a lot and the time was beneficial for my merchandising job. It also allowed me to form a bond with the people in the plant, a friendship that would help me in the future.

I was now back in Atlanta doing my new job in the corporate world where things moved slowly and in a bureaucratic way. In many cases, the process was more important than the results. I remember one situation where I was trying to get the JC Penny shirt size requirement for the next line of merchandise to send to our manufacturing plant. I asked our Account Representative in New York for the needed information several times with no results. The urgency was that we needed a certain amount of time for manufacturing so we could get the shirts on the shelves in time for their intended next sales event. Since the process was stressful, the approach I used was to send the Account Representative a memo every time we talked stressing the urgency of getting the shirt size mix. My frustration was building, and the deadline was days away, I escalated the issue to my boss and he in turn escalated it up the corporate hierarchy. After much pointing of fingers, blaming our client, and alibiing, I got the shirt size mix I needed. The outcome was we were just able to get the shirts made and on the shelves on time. Afterward my boss gave me some good advice, "If you don't get a response after two tries, escalate." "Otherwise, you will take the heat for someone else's screw up."

In this situation, I learned to communicate up the line with the first sign of an issue, and I learned not to abandon my core values (of getting results) while taking a more bureaucratic approach. Another lesson in being nice but tough.

My family life had also changed. Sam and I had purchased our first house, a sixteen hundred square foot tri-level, three bedroom, one and a half bath with a carport at the purchase price of $28,500. In May of the next year, Sam gave birth to our beautiful daughter, Jennifer. The labor itself was interesting because Sam was a nurse at the hospital where Jennifer was born. We went to the hospital late in the evening and upon check-in there was a steady stream of nurses coming in to visit her. I learned many lessons about childbirth; besides the usual ones, two others stand out, first make sure you have plenty of gas in the car and not have to stop for gas like I did, and second, you don't need to pack a bunch of underwear for your wife's hospital stay.

At this point in my career, I wanted to get back into Human Resources. It was July and I contacted several the headhunters I knew in Atlanta, one of those contacts called me about a job as the Southeast Regional Human Resources manager for Bonanza Steakhouses, a casual dining restaurant chain based in Dallas, Texas. The restaurant chain had been started by Dan Blocker, "Hoss" Cartwright on the TV Series Bonanza, in 1963.

I told the headhunter I was interested; he arranged a phone interview with Bonanza's VP of Human Resources. I took the call a couple days later and it went so well I was invited to Dallas for a face-to-face interview. That took a lot of pressure off since I had limited experience in Human Resources, and I didn't know if I could land an interview. I knew I wasn't interviewing with a Fortune 100 company, but it was a chance to gain experience and get back on that career path. The Dallas interview went well, and I was hired. I was to return to Dallas in two weeks to start my restaurant training, and I gave my resignation with two weeks' notice to Oxford.

On the designated date I flew to Dallas, reported to the corporate offices, and began my training. On my second day I was called to CEO[15] Web Lowe's office, I didn't know what to think. Had I screwed up on my first day? But it wasn't that at all. He made it a point of meeting new employees to welcome them to the company and share his vision of the company. One question he asked was, "are you a runner?" I said I wasn't, and he suggested I get a pair of shoes and start running. He apologized for not having a pair of running shoes in his office to give me, apparently something he did. "I want my management to be healthy and have an outlet for the stress the job places on them," he said. Web Lowe also knew the benefits running brought because had been an avid runner for years. He was considered by everyone to be a gentleman and his experience in the food service industry started with a job at McDonalds in high school. He considered himself a born entrepreneur and had started several successful food service companies. His job at Bonanza was to build the company with a combination of company-owned and franchise stores. I was happy that I'd gotten the job at Bonanza so I could be a part of building a successful company and to be able to work with Web Lowe, a charismatic visionary. During my time with the company Web met, as he says, a beautiful blonde on a flight and they knew they were meant for each other. Her name was Ruta Lee, an actor in movies and TV. They dated and got married shortly after I left the company.

After my training I went back to Atlanta and got to work on my first assignment which was to start the search for a new company office. The current one, in Atlanta, only had one enclosed office for the Regional Manager and everyone else worked in one common area. Also, the office wasn't in a great part of town. Corporate management and our franchise sales team wanted a place that looked good to meet with prospective

---

[15] A Chief Executive Officer is the highest officer charged with the management of an organization.

franchisees. It took a couple of months to find a suitable office option and get our real-estate department to sign off on it. Once that was done, I started working with the landlord on the build out, which took another three months. It was finally completed, we moved in, and my mission was accomplished. But building out a new office was a minor part of my job.

My real job was building a region of the company staffed with solid talent. To do so would mean extensive travel, something I hadn't done before, and little did I know that while visiting every store in the region and getting to know the managers and crews I was starting a business life of extensive travel.

I had done research on the casual dining and fast-food industries before coming on board and what I found was going to be a challenge. They were known as renegades in a cutthroat business. The most challenging was the lack of experienced and trained managers. The business wouldn't be considered by Fortune 100 executives as sophisticated, but they wouldn't know the long hours, high employee turnover, theft, cost control, and customer satisfaction issues facing the managers. You might say, well, that's their job, so they should be able to handle it. But remember most of the managers had to learn their job without formal training or the luxury of getting up to speed. They usually jump in the deep end and must perform.

I had many occasions when I would lock heads with a district manager or area manager because they would hire a friend of a friend and not follow the process of not doing full references and background checks or get a second opinion interview. The second area of concern for me was the rumors about managers forcing employees to have sex with them, even in the restaurant's freezer, I hoped it was not true in this company.

On a store trip to Greensboro, North Carolina I was hit with an unsettling situation. I arrived at the store at 10 a.m., met the store manager and decided to get an early lunch before the store got busy with the lunch crowd. I got my lunch and sat down at a booth to eat when two young ladies, crew members, came over and sat across from me in the booth. I introduced myself and they did as well. Their introduction included them laughing and pointing out to me they were twins, which was obvious. When I'm in a store, I met with as many crew members as I could, so this was on opportunity to talk to two of them. We chatted and I ask how things were going in the store and other standard questions. They said they were happy with the work and the managers. Before getting up from the booth they want to know one thing, "Do you want us to sleep with you like we've done with others?" My stomach immediately turned over and I felt sick. I looked at them straight in the eye "No that's not a requirement, and it shouldn't be a requirement of any manager." "Okay" they said, giggled and left the booth. I couldn't finish my meal but sat there for a while to calm down. I decided to wait until after the lunch rush before talking to the store manager about my conversation with the young ladies. I completed all my checklist of things to do and met with him to do a recap before departing for the airport. During my recap I asked his opinion about my earlier conversation with the two ladies. He waited a few seconds before answering. When he did, he just said these two ladies were a little wacky and I shouldn't consider it an issue. I wasn't sure if I should buy his explanation, so upon return to Atlanta I talked to the regional and district managers as well. They said they weren't concerned either. I never discovered the true answer. It could've been that I was the butt of a joke, being the new guy.

Web Lowe was replaced by John Teets, another professional leader who I admired. John was also an avid exerciser and hard worker. His background was that he started working in the food industry at age fourteen. His experience as at Greyhound Corporation, which is a division of ITT before coming to Bonanza. His style was much like Harold Geneen, CEO of ITT Corporation. Both knew every detail of their businesses and industry.

When we had our monthly and quarterly business review meetings with John Teets, it could be a good meeting or turn out to be brutal. First the table in the room was shaped in a U with John and his only assistant at the closed end of the U. There was one seat in the middle of the U and that was for the individual whose operation was being reviewed. Success at the meeting was simple, know your operation, don't try to cover up issues or talk your way out of poor performance, and don't point the finger at anyone else including your own managers. If you came in and knew how your operation was performing and why, as well as where your operation wasn't performing, and why, and what your plan was to fix it, your part of the meeting would go well. If you came in and didn't know your operation, you were in for a bad day. I remember one fellow who did all the wrong things and was basically a clown. John started asking questions that he, John, knew the answers to but the fellow on the hot seat didn't. It only took a few minutes for John to devastate him. After he dismissed him, he paused for about thirty seconds and apologized to the rest of us for what had just happened. All John wanted was for his managers and executives to do their job as professionals. That is what his mentor, Harold Geneen had expected of him.

I caught my share of heat when our stores were short on management and John expected me to solve the problem. John wanted me, Human Resources, to bring in the needed managers and this was still a work in progress because the District and Area managers wanted to do their own recruiting.

While I was working for Bonanza, my dad and a partners purchased two Bonanza steakhouse franchises in Asheville and Hendersonville, North Carolina. And continued to operate the stores for several years after I left Bonanza.

I learned a lot during my time at Bonanza and had a chance to get back into Human Resources. I learned the potentially seedy side of business. I learned the tragic side when one of our store managers on Cleveland Avenue in Atlanta was killed one morning before the store opened. A gunman wanting to rob the store forced his way in and during the robbery, killed our manager. I also learned how to be a professional, a gentleman, tough minded, and physically and mentally solid. I had had two examples of CEO's that I couldn't have wanted better coaches.

CHAPTER 7

FINDING PASSION

I was back on my career path. One day a friend of mine, who was a contract recruiter, called me about a new job opportunity with Frito-Lay. I said yes immediately because of their size and professional reputation. After an initial phone conversation, they invited me to fly to Dallas, Texas, for an interview for an open position in corporate Human Resources.

The trip was scheduled to be a day trip, flying from Atlanta to Dallas allowed me to start my day in Dallas early morning their time because of gaining an hour due to the time zone change. Upon arriving at their corporate headquarters and I was met by a company recruiter who went over my schedule. My day started immediately with the first of several interviews and ended with the Senior Vice President of Human Resources. "Are you open to staying in Atlanta for a Human Resources position at our plant?" he asked toward the end of the interview. He explained they just had an opening at the Atlanta manufacturing plant that morning and my interview was timely. I told him that I was open to remain in Atlanta, and we finished our interview, shook hands, and I was escorted into the Director of Recruiting's office. The Director of Recruiting explained the Atlanta position and with no relocation to Dallas, which would work well for both of us. We agreed on the offer, terms, and a start date. I left for the Dallas-Fort Worth airport where I called Sam to tell her about the good news before boarding a plane back to Atlanta.

The Director of Recruiting had filled me in on the background of the Atlanta plant which held a soft spot in the heart of everyone in the company. The plant had always been the flagship, with many top executives spending their early careers there. The executives were embarrassed that this plant was now posting "poor performance," a situation that couldn't be allowed to stand, so the company was bringing in a new plant manager and a new Human Resources team. I knew going in that it would require hard work and carried with it high visibility. My plan was simple, I needed to spend time on the plant floor finding out details of the operation and searching for what was wrong, that would mean talking to the employees, supervisors, and managers getting their perspective and ideas.

My start date as the Plant Assistant Human Resources Manager was two weeks later. Which gave me time for a little rest and to mentally adjust to the task ahead. On my first day, I met with the Plant Manager and the Plant Human Resources Manager, my boss, and asked their permission to spend the next two weeks working on all three shifts in all departments and to ride a couple of delivery trucks. That would give me a chance to do a deep dive into plant operations and maybe get some ideas about the problems and how to fix them. They both quickly agreed, and I was on my way.

The first department I visited was one that consistently didn't meet their performance goals. My meeting was scheduled for 7:00 AM, the beginning of first shift, I introduced myself to the shift manager and explain that my objective was to get to know the operation and get his views on what could help. "I know we aren't making our goals," he said. "And the reason is that the employees are just not capable enough or don't want to produce the results needed." "I don't know what you will find that will help because the employees are the problem, and I can't do anything about it because they're unionized." I listened to him and just said that we would see what we could find out.

I left his office and went to the production line where the raw materials came in and followed the process through to where the snack food products were bagged. I didn't see anything in the line flow to this point to suggest that improvement was needed, mainly because it was mostly automated. In the bagging section I introduced myself to an operator and asked if I could observe and asking for his suggestions on improving the process. "Also, if you have any suggestions for improvements, that would be great," I said. He agreed, and I positioned myself next to the bagging machine and tried to stay out of his way. I asked him to explain the bagging process and what his job was as it was told to him. He complied, and his explanation seemed straight forward. But, while we were talking, I noticed something that seemed a bit odd. The operator's technique, as he explained it, was to let the spool of bags get down to a certain level and switch the line to the second roll of bags already hung and ready to go. That way, he could do what management had told him to do which, wasn't to let the line go down by running out of bags. When the operator switched to the second roll, it looked like there were quite a few bags left on the spool. I continued to observe him through two more roll changeovers. Each time he switched the line at a point he thought was correct and threw the almost spent rolls in the garbage can. I knew that the bags were expensive and made up a large portion of the product cost, I asked him if I could take the old rolls from the garbage. "Sure, it's trash," he said. I thanked him and asked again if he had any suggestions, he didn't.

Later that morning, when the department manager came in, I went into his office and asked him how short the department was from making their performance goals. After he went through a couple of reports, he gave me the answer. I showed him the old rolls of bags and asked him to calculate the cost of the discarded bags. He estimated the cost and then stated, "if these bags hadn't been discarded early, I could've consistently met or exceeded my department's goals."

The department manager and I agreed that additional training of the bag operators was in order. That agreement was a good opening, I next shared my conversations with the employees where I learned they were in the dark about department performance expectations. All they knew was that supervisors would have a meeting to tell them if the department met or didn't meet the performance goals. They were given a bunch of numbers that were meaningless. If the goals weren't met, in this case that was most of the time, the supervisor would come around and tell them to work harder. "Well, I guess we're just not getting through to them," the manager said. I suggested more in-depth training along with the periodic meetings that asked for the employees help and suggestions on how to improve the departments performance. "We can give it a try, nothing else is working," he said. At this point, I suggested that we see the plant manager and update him on our findings. We proceeded up the stairs to his office, where we shared our findings, and I made sure that the department manager got equal credit for finding the solutions. The solution, I reiterated, while still giving the department manager credit, was to start an education program to teach the employees not only the "what" of their performance scores, but the why." The employees needed the complete picture because they would be the ones implementing the solution and would be the ones who could come up with suggestions for improvement. This also would help to mend the split between employees and management that had started years before when the employees voted in favor of union representation.

The plant manager agreed, and we put together an education program for this department and started with our first employee meeting the next week. The education program included explaining in detail the goals for the company, plant, and department. We asked the employees for their input on how to achieve those goals and created an interactive team environment by opening the communication. The performance of this department soon improved to where they were consistently achieving their goals and, in many cases, exceeding them.

I continued my journey through each department in the plant and found many opportunities for improvement, the two consistent themes were the employees lack of understanding of performance goals and the split between management and employees, which caused indifference on both sides. Since the education and communication program worked so well in the first department, we took it plant-wide with the same great results. After a few months of improved performance, the word reached corporate, and they wanted to know the details of the program. After sending them the plan and answering questions, they took it and rolled out to other plants, resulting in a performance boost, in the company. I was elated because this is the reason, I'd gotten into a management career. Yes, the pats on the back were great, but it was getting results that was the reward.

Unfortunately, during my deep dive in the departments, I uncovered some management practices that weren't acceptable, including poor treatment of employees. In one department, I observed a production line where the employees sat to perform the quality inspection of the product before bagging as opposed to the others where the employee stood. I asked the supervisor the reason and he said it was because the line was so low the employees would otherwise have to bend over their whole shift. The next night, I went back for my in-depth observation. As I walked to the line, I saw the employees weren't sitting to perform their quality inspections, they were standing and bending over the line to perform their inspections. I asked the supervisor why the employees weren't sitting, and he said that they had made him mad the previous day and this was their punishment. His statement punched me in my gut. I asked him if his manager was okay with this approach. "I run my line the way I want to get performance," he said.

I completed my observation but didn't go home after this third shift was over. Instead, I waited for the plant manager to come to work so I could meet with him. In our meeting, I explained what had happened and he, too, was appalled. He said he would address it immediately and I could go home to get sleep, but I went across the street for breakfast to return afterword. During that time the plant manager met with the supervisor who confessed what had happened.

After breakfast I went back by the plant manager's office, and he told me he took care of the issue quickly by terminating the supervisor on the spot. In doing so, the plant manager reinforced his commitment to build a team, work with the employees and not just boss them around. His action had a ripple effect among all levels of the plant's management. They now knew he was serious and that I was there as part of a new team to help improve the operation. However, some of them were guarded when I came to their department, yet others knew I had helped several departments to improve their performance and were at ease working with me. Either reaction was okay with me because I felt we were improving the plant's performance, improving the working conditions of our employees, and building a team environment for sustained success. These three things were a part of my core values, and I included them to my newly created notebook on how to improve performance. A notebook where I continued to add good practices and over many years became my manual.

In this case, I employed both previously learned and new lessons. First, my father had taught me to go to the people who did the work to learn what is really going on. Second, he taught me that there is enough credit to go around, and not try to take all of it myself. Third, I learned that consistent open communication between all levels in an organization is vital.

Frito-Lay also gave me the opportunity to work on contract negotiations preparation with the Teamsters and Bakers unions in Detroit, Michigan. My assignment was to pull together the data, analysis, and other information to assist our negotiating team. The Teamsters contract starts with the signing of a national Master Freight Agreement between a "target" company and the Teamsters. That agreement was then taken forward by the Teamster to other companies with the expectations it will be agreed to as well. Although while those subsequent companies end up mostly signing the national agreement there are specific items each company negotiates pertaining to their business needs. The data for those specific items is what I was charged to assemble. To do the assignment I traveled to Detroit where most of the data was that I needed. The comical part was that I was sent in the dead of winter from a warmer southern location, wearing only light weight clothing and taking a light raincoat which meant I froze my back side off. The locals got a big laugh out of this "hick" coming in ill prepared for the snow and ice. The work I did was good and that did earn me some respect even though my cloths didn't.

My tenure at Frito Lay didn't last long. Because of the success at the Atlanta plant, I was asked to move to Bingham, New York for the purpose of improving that plant's performance. I agreed to visit the Bingham plant and decide, along with my wife, after my return. My plant visit was in the middle of winter, and upon my arrival, it was cold with twenty-two inches of snow on the ground and more forecast. Not a positive introduction to Bingham for a guy living in Georgia. I talked with the plant manager who was pitching the assignment and several of the plant management staff, who were happy there and didn't want to move around to fill the company's needs. But when I met with the current Human Resources Manager, I discovered he desperately wanted to move out of that location. Unfortunately, a few people had been transferred in, didn't like it, and found it was almost impossible to transfer out. It seems that no one in the company wanted to move there and recruiting from the outside was hard as well. My possible transfer now appeared to be filling a slot and not to improve performance, something that was both disappointing and deflating. I flew back to Atlanta, talked it over with Sam, notified the company that I declined the transfer.

When the word got around, I was told by some fellow managers who had been with the company for many years that I needed to take the transfer because not taking it would severely limit my advancement within the company and could lead to my replacement. I didn't know if this was true, but my previous experience with Dad being forced to move at the Army's discretion, and its hardships, came to mind. I still declined the move and asked my immediate manager what impact it would have on my career. He told me not to worry—everything would be okay. Being told not to worry didn't help, I still felt a heavy cloud over me, and my instinct kept telling me my future wasn't secure, so I started looking for other career opportunities outside the company. I was disappointed because I was passionate about the work I had done at Frito-Lay.

My next position was as the Human Resources Manager at the Research & Development Center for Celanese in Charlotte, North Carolina. My job was interesting because the Ph.D.'s and engineers at the center were creative and challenging people.

Sam and I had purchased a dark brown two-story house in Pineville, NC, which was south of Charlotte, about twenty minutes away from work. The house was new, and it had a heat pump installed. My first time in a house with a heat pump. The builder said he also had wrapped the house in plastic to maintain a more even temperature year-round. The house sat on a treeless lot, because the builder had stripped all the trees down in the development and of course planted a couple of starter trees. As it turned out the house was hot in the summer and chilly in the winter. The house wrapping caused moisture to be held inside and helped mildew to grow. The house wasn't horrible, but it had challenges.

One day not long after we announced our annual promotions, a mechanical engineer came to my office with a complaint. He was upset because he hadn't been promoted. His frustration was clearly high. In these cases, I listened and asked questions to see if I could find out the root of the problem. I asked him if he had talked to his manager. He said yes, and was told his work was acceptable, but not exceptional. We continued to talk, and I asked him why he thought he should've been promoted. After thinking for moment and answered, "Well, I just should've." We continued to talk for a while longer and it was obvious to me that we weren't going to solve the problem that day.

My instincts told me to dig deeper. I scheduled another meeting for the following week. We met several more times and I tried several ways to get at to the root of his issue, but he continued to deflect. Finally, he said that he thought he should've been promoted because his fellow employees thought he deserved the promotion. He still didn't answer the question as to why *he* thought he should've gotten it. In our next session, he said that his wife thought he should've been promoted. Now we have both peer and family pressures about his lack of a promotion. I continued to dig, "Why do you think you deserved the promotion?" "Well, I don't know," he blurted out, "I really don't like the job anyway." My next question was, "What would you rather be doing?" He didn't hesitate and responded by saying that he would love to be an engineer in the world of NASCAR. When I asked why, he went into detail about why and what he liked about working in that world. I then asked why he hadn't pursued that path, he said that his family and his co-workers wouldn't understand. It took a couple more sessions before he decided to talk to his family and manager about his dream.

A few months later, he came by my office to tell me he was leaving Celanese to take an engineering job on the NASCAR circuit. He and I were both excited that he now had a chance to follow his dream. I didn't have contact with him after that to see if it was working out, but his passion told me he would be successful.

In business, I see many workers who feel trapped in situations they don't think they can do anything about. Their focus seems to be making it to the next holiday, vacation, or in some cases to retirement. They may have knowledge, and even be successful, but they don't have passion, focus, concentration, or fun. High-performing companies must have an atmosphere and culture of passion and success. Without that, it's another assembly line churning out stuff. The culture of success must start at the top, the executive ranks. But even when that culture exists, it doesn't mean that everyone is cut out for the work they're doing or the company they're with. The most successful career plan is to learn what we're good at doing and what company environment you like. Something that isn't easy to do, and it may take several tries to get it right, but when it happens it's the best place to be for a happy life.

The Celanese department managers felt that their knowledge, skills, and experience in management were at a level they didn't need or see the value in help from the Human Resources function. As time went on my workdays were spent calculating statistics, helping with presentations, and other administrative tasks—not the impactful work I had at Frito-Lay.

I kept thinking of the engineer who finally figured out his passion and had to ask myself, had I? My job was okay but a bit boring, and I missed Atlanta which led me to be receptive to any job opportunities. My constant moves, in military life, made it easy for me to consider another move. My family wasn't as enthusiastic.

CHAPTER 8

TIME FOR CHANGE

Once again, I received a call from a headhunter friend saying that Coca-Cola USA in Atlanta was starting a new recruiting function and was looking for an experienced Human Resources manager to get it going and run it. I talked with Sam and decided to interview for the position. Charlotte was an okay place to live but we liked Atlanta. As luck would have it, a friend who was working in the recruiting function for Coca-Cola Corporate gave me a good reference, which helped me get the job.

The Chairman of Coca-Cola was J Paul Austin, a person that I began to admire as I learned more about his accomplishments. He had started in the legal department at Coke in 1949, and from 1950 to 1958 he had worked in various leadership positions in the Coca-Cola Export Corporation. He spent several years in Johannesburg, South Africa overseeing Coca-Cola's operations in Africa. He returned to Atlanta in 1958 and became Chairman in 1970. In that role he significantly grew Coca-Cola's export markets. He brought Coke to countries where it hadn't been in the past or where it had even been boycotted. He launched Fanta Orange in the Soviet Union, where Pepsi's had a monopoly at the time. Pepsi's entry into the Soviet Union reportedly, although denied, helped by their relationship with President Richard Nixon, which resulted in a temporary monopoly. Austin continued his goal of expanding globally, and by holding meetings and developing relationships with country leaders, he restored operations in the previously boycotted countries of Egypt, Yemen, and Sudan. Coke had struggled in the

Middle East, because of a boycott by the Arab League, as punishment for it selling in Israel.

One of my assignments as Recruiting Manager was to seek out and recruit students attending Georgia Tech, University of Georgia, and other local schools who were from these and other countries where Coke was seeking reentry. We wanted to get people into the company that were knowledgeable about those countries to work in Coke to learn the company's values, vision, and products, and who could help in the work to relaunch it in those countries. It's a hard sell in a country if you don't understand the people and culture, and Austin knew that firsthand.

Those of us working in the Atlanta offices of Coke knew that Austin was making many trips to China in the hopes of regaining assess to that country. It also seemed that on every trip, he came back with tons of Chinese art. Those trips, and his ability to form relationships, resulted in his December 1978 announcement that Coca-Cola would return to China after a 30-year ban and that importation would start in 1979. Coke was introduced into China in 1927 and was a popular drink until the Chinese Civil War in1949. The conclusion of the civil war, the communist took control of mainland China, forming the People's Republic of China. At that point importation of Coke was stopped because it was perceived as a symbol of a decadent capitalist lifestyle—a Western culture.

It's also significant that a few days after Coke's announcement, President Carter announced the normalization of relations between the United States and China. Coca-Cola has maintained there wasn't a connection.

I noted earlier that Pepsi had supposedly had a relationship with President Richard Nixon and J Paul Austin was a supporter of Jimmy Carter during his 1976 campaign with his contributions and introductions to influential people. I also know that some members of the Carter family, friends, and political relationships were employed by Coca-Cola for a while. These employments weren't unusual at Coke because we employed various family members of Coke Bottlers and other individuals who helped form business relationships. This approach is also common in many corporations.

Another assignment was to build an MBA summer intern program focusing on Harvard's MBA School. Since J Paul Austin had gone to Harvard, the pressure was significant. My recruiting team and I put together a well done and complete program. I arranged the interviews, at Harvard with the school's administration and set off for Boston. My schedule included short interviews with students who were interested in a summer internship with Coke—well, at least I *thought* they were. During my interviews I found out that the school had made up the schedule and chose the students for the interviews.

After reflecting on the interviews, I was disappointed in the talent. I had expected more in terms of knowledge, drive, and professionalism. What I saw was students who felt they were entitled to invitations to visit the companies' headquarters and join our summer intern program. They felt this was just a way of letting *them* decide where they wanted to work and not the company. After the interviews, I invited all the interviewees to visit our headquarter in Atlanta, but only a half dozen accepted.

When the time came for their trip to Atlanta, I pulled out all the stops—interviews with the top executives, tours of our operations, and a great dinner with key executives serving Cokes and Sterling wines, a soon to be acquired company. After all that no, I repeat, zero of the students accepted our offer of a summer internship. The feedback I got was they wanted to go to a more prestigious company. Coke was a good place to work. It was exciting with the global expansion and the ongoing search for other good companies to buy. I was disappointed that the students didn't see it that way.

My challenges as the new recruitment manager were that Coke hadn't had this function in the past. The belief among most of the executives and some of the managers was that Coke was so well-known and so beloved that people lined up to work with the company. The actual act of recruiting seemed unnatural or even offensive. But many of the managers, supervisors and a few executives who had to get the job done knew better. My key internal customers were the executives, and if they didn't believe Coke needed this new recruiting function, then it wouldn't work.

I agreed that overall, Coke was a good place to work, but leaving the talent acquisition to chance wasn't the best for future growth, as my assignment of recruiting foreign students to further Cokes global expansion clearly showed. Another challenge was starting a new function from scratch—office, people, processes, and more. And my biggest challenge was me. When I take on a new job or assignment, I fully engage, some of the time too forcefully. Usually when a new function is launched it has the blessing of top management and that's communicated throughout the company, but that didn't seem to be the case here. I called many executives to introduce myself only to hear, "who are you and what do you do?" I understand that as an outsider I will see things and issues more clearly than those who have been inside the company for a while. But I also know that I need to spend time immersing myself in the culture to be successful.

During my time at Coke, I was going through a bad phase in my life, in my marriage and I was drinking too much after work. Those things meant I wasn't ready or willing to do the job of selling this new recruiting function. I expected complete compliance from everyone at Coke. But that didn't happen and my tenure there was short lived.

Next up, I accepted a position with Eckerd Drugs as the District Human Resources manager based in Birmingham, Alabama covering seventy stores in that state, Florida, and Tennessee. At Eckerd I was back traveling again, something I hadn't done much at Frito-Lay, Celanese or Coke. I was now spending many nights in motels or hotels, eating out, and drinking, then going to bed. This was a constant weekly cycle because the territory was spread out and the employee population dispersed. I traveled by company car—stripped-down version of a mid-sized sedan, black wall tires and small hubcaps that only covered the lug nuts. It only had a radio, so I installed a cassette player and speakers to listen to my music. Looking at the car your first reaction would be, this is a government car. Luckily, that's what the Alabama Highway Patrol thought when I would travel the interstate especially with our security manager, both of us in white shirts and ties. When they passed us going either way, they would signal a hello, which I returned.

Occasionally, when the executives from our corporate offices in Florida would tour stores, I flew with them in the company Beechcraft King Air twin-turboprop airplane. But being lowest in rank I had to sit in the back of the plane in a small single seat, the area that seemed to get most of the ups, downs, lefts, and rights. I was also the place where the beer cooler was stashed, and I became the bartender. However, there was no alcohol until the senior executive on the plane declared the workday had ended. The policy at Eckerd was no alcohol until after work. Sometimes that was a problem when I was on the road because I would go to dinner and have a drink and get a call to come back to a store. In those cases, I broke company policy, and I even felt guilty when I went on vacation and had wine at lunch.

My job was a typical human resources role with some not so usual daily events. The company had a policy to use polygraphs, and every new hire had to take one and once a year every employee had to take one. I wasn't sold on their use because

I felt it was an insult to good employee relations. Also, taking them was intimidating because one of the questions as was, "Have you ever broken any company policy?" My answer had to be "yes" even if I hadn't gone back to a store after dinner, I'd probably broken some company policy somewhere. The response from my manager was, "John, we've all broken policies so just answer no." It didn't make sense.

I remember one cashier who was caught taking $2 from the register. When we pulled the polygraphs there was no indication of this infraction. But when I questioned her, the response was, "well I was due a five cents per hour raise two years ago and I felt that I was wrongfully denied that raise, so I take out $2 every week to make up for it." This person felt taking the money was justified so it didn't show up on the test.

Discrimination against employees was on everyone's mind locally and nationally. I received several discrimination complaints during my time at Eckerd, and I investigated each one and found most had no foundation—they were just a result of disciplinary problems the employee was trying to circumvent. There were a few where the proper internal steps weren't followed, and I pulled back the action taken to the previous step that was skipped. There was only one where termination occurred, and my investigation showed that action had been inappropriate. In that case, the employee was reinstated with back pay. I was pleased that with the number of cases I investigated, our managers did a good job by taking the right steps considering what I was hearing about other industries and companies.

Store management recruitment was a major undertaking. The store management were what is known as working managers. That means other than cashiers and a cosmetics person, they had to do the work of stocking shelves, unloading trucks, doing aisle resets, setting out promotional signs and banners, sales, cash, and reports. The heavy load and long hours caused a high turnover, so my job was to recruit, screen and hire the talent needed. The candidate pipeline was by ads, referrals from area managers and other store managers, and occasionally walk-ins. The selection process required each candidate to participate with the other candidate in a half day of role playing and various exercises, while being evaluated by several members of the district's management. I usually had a seasoned store manager, and one to two area managers. The program was a good selection tool and better than just individual interviews and opinions. It was, however, a bit more complex than the situation required. For each event, I had to take the lead of running the day, conducting the evaluation session at the end of the day, and any follow up items. We had a result on each candidate before we departed, so the next step could be taken by each area manager. These events were scheduled for one per month and the calendar was set for the entire year, no changes.

At the time of one event, Sam was scheduled for surgery, and I wanted to be at the hospital. I brought my assistant to the event to help me juggle things and possibly allow me to go to the hospital, a few blocks away. I did manage to slip away one time during the event but caught hell for doing so. The philosophy at the time in business required total loyalty to the company, even over family. I should've insisted on a replacement for that one event, rather than trying to do everything myself.

There was one dramatic incident that happened when I was sent to the Atlanta Regional office and warehouse to fill in for my boss who was going on vacation. I arrived one morning the day before he was to leave. He and I had an update meeting so I could carry on in his absence. Afterwards, he went home to start packing for his departure later that day. Next, I decided to get the feel and layout of the warehouse, so I left the office and proceeded to walk the warehouse and introduce myself to the managers and employees. After an hour, I stopped to talk to a warehouse worker, and after a couple of minutes, he informed me that later that day a union would be coming in to notify the company that they were filing papers to have an election for union representation of our employees. If what he said was true, it would be an event that would cause sudden and large-scale turmoil to the company—one that isn't seen in the southern United States who have the right to work laws that don't require employees to join a union, even if one has been elected to represent them, so employees have no need to vote in favor of union representation.

I thanked the employee for this information and immediately went to the office to hopefully catch my boss before he left for vacation. I was able to talk to him on the phone and he was back at the warehouse within thirty minutes. We called our corporate office in Florida to let our Vice President of Human Resources and Director of Employee Relations know what was going on. The director said he would be on the next plane to Atlanta and see us the next morning. The union did partition for an election, and we went into union prevention mode.

Usually, either one of two scenarios brings the unionization attempt. First, there could be a union, mole inside the employee ranks to sell the employees on unionization, or the company is treating employees so badly that they band together and seek unionization. We needed to find out if it was one of these two situations or something else. I was given the task of going back to do a reference check all the new-hire employees within the last year. It only took me a couple of days and I found our union infiltrator, which meant someone in our regional Human Resources office hadn't properly checked references. With the knowledge of who our union infiltrator was, we could then dig further to uncover information to tell us the issues, their severity, and extent of the problem. We discovered the original disgruntled employee was in the pharmacist group, and the mole in the warehouse was designed to bring that population of employees into the pro-union fold. With that information we could quickly narrow down the pharmacists who had frequently complained and the substance of those complaints. There were only a few complainers, and their issues seemed unreasonable. But at least we had a better understanding of the facts.

After some time and legal back and forth, a union certification vote was scheduled. The day came, votes were cast, and the union lost. In addition, the warehouse union infiltrator quit immediately after the vote, and the primary pharmacist complainer eventually found a job with another company. I can understand how people can become unhappy with their companies, as I've done that have and deciding to leave the company. But overall Eckerd Drugs was not a bad place to work.

In September of 1979 Hurricane Frederic hit the panhandle coast which included Mobile, Alabama. The hurricane had 145 mile per hour winds, caused five deaths and $2.3 billion in damage. We had several stores sustain damages, which required our management and private security to go and stand guard. In each store our pharmacies contained inventories of drugs worth a lot of money, and some were controlled substances that didn't need to find their way into the general population. I went on site as well, but my role had more to do with employee support.

A couple more unusual incidences involved store employees being terminated by the local store manager who had proper approvals up the line for their actions. Both contained elements of race and outside influences. The first one started when I got a call from the sheriff's office to inform me a picketing permit had been approved for one of our stores in the Birmingham area. The demonstration was scheduled because a Black manager had terminated a white employee, and the Ku Klux Klan was objecting. The group would be picketing that following Saturday, I checked the files, and our independent shopping team found that this employee had improperly rang a sale, which was automatic grounds for termination. Our procedure was that from time to time our shopping team would go into the store and make a cash purchase, with the exact amount including tax. They would then wait for a regular customer to go through and check out. Then the second shopping team member would make a purchase. If the employee hadn't rung up the first sale and deposited the cash in the register by the time of the second shopping team purchase, this was considered an improper ringing of a sale resulting in termination.

Saturday came, and our security manager and I were in the store when the Ku Klux Klan members came in with their white full-length robes and white pointed hats, but their faces weren't covered. They walked around, went to the check out, bought something small, and left. Of course, there were reporters with microphones and cameras outside. Neither I nor any Eckerd employees made any comments, and there wasn't a reversal of the termination.

Within a month I received a call from a politician in Selma, Alabama protesting the termination of a Black employee by a white store manager. Again, I checked the file, and it was the same situation where the shopping team caught an employee improperly ringing a sale. The politician wanted a meeting in Selma. I agreed and set up one in a meeting room at the local Holiday Inn. As before, both our security manager and I traveled to Selma for the meeting. As we walked into the meeting room, there were six other people in addition to the politician. The politician did all the talking, and after some time and discussion, my position was still firm. The employee was correctly terminated for a policy infraction, and no other reason. The termination would stand.

The meeting ended, we shook hands and left. "Do you know who those people were around the table", my security manager asked? I replied that I didn't. "They were people who marched across the bridge with Dr. Martin Luther King" he further stated. I was embarrassed that I hadn't recognized them and mad that these people, who had given so much already, had been pulled into this meeting when the politician had obviously not gotten the facts about this case before pursuing it and was trying to further his political career. My embarrassment and anger aside, nothing else ever came of the politician's complaint.

My time with Eckerd's was certainly eventful, and my family enjoyed living in Birmingham, Alabama. But time passed, and an opportunity to join Unijax in Jacksonville, Florida as an Employee Relations manager arose. Jacksonville is a large city in terms of size, the county is the city, and population of 614,000, at the time. I took the job, and our family moved there at a time when interest rates were in the eighteen percent range. We bought a house by assuming the current loan and got a high interest rate for the balance of the purchase price. The house was in the Beauclerc area south of the city and was a red antique brick ranch style with three bedrooms, two baths, formal living room, and den and was built in 1970. It was picturesque with the ranch house nestled among the Live Oak and hanging Spanish Moss trees and a couple blocks off the St. Johns River. Unfortunately, the public schools in Florida were poor so Sam and I decided to send Jennifer to a private school. A bit costly but necessary and of course worth it. Jacksonville was an enjoyable city with costal beauty, warm and cold weather, beaches, and a pleasant life. However, my extensive travel schedule was taxing.

My job was to improve the employee experience, give input on how to improve company policies pertaining to employees, conduct training, address employee complaints, investigate workplace situations and rules violations, and collect and analyze a lot of data.

The company was growing with several acquisitions of similar companies resulting in many reorganizations. In one reorganization I was promoted to Human Resources manager covering fourteen branch locations and the corporate office. I became totally responsible for all aspect of the human resources function in those locations which in some locations had both union and non-union employees.

My travel was impacted by living in Jacksonville because air travel meant going through Atlanta to complete my trips. That connection increased my travel time by a few hours each way or longer if there were delays in Atlanta or along the route. I developed a weekly routine that when I arrived back in Jacksonville and left the airport or office work on Fridays, I put the top down on my MG and didn't put it up again until Monday morning. That gave me a sense of freedom and helped put the issues of the week behind me. I also took up racquetball, as another escape, and played daily when I wasn't traveling.

In addition to the normal tasks, I reviewed new initiatives in the company to project the human resources impact. One program that was proposed included the company starting our own trucking lines. This would pick up products from suppliers and redistribute to our locations and save money by not using third party transporters. Upon my review I noticed the projected pay rates for the drivers was low compared to the market. When I questioned the rates and was told, "We must have those rates for this idea to make money" by the operations management. I made the case that with low wages this left us open for high turnover, employee morale issues and ripe for unionization. All of these would necessitate moving to higher rates, which would negate projected profits and would require serious financial expenditure. The operations management didn't like me throwing cold water on their idea but after much heated discussion the company scrapped the idea.

My new responsibilities included working with the unions in a few locations. One such location was where two different Teamster Locals represented our employees, one had the truckers, and one had the warehouse. The two unions refused to work together, work with management and constantly filed grievances.

Their behavior negatively impacted the distribution operation and was unacceptable. The company needed this resolved so I went in to meet with both unions. My message was straightforward, their antics were costing the company money, and they needed to start working with each other, company management, stop filing grievances for every little thing that came up, and stop slowing down on the job. I also reminded them that each location is constantly being evaluated for its financial viability and they're negatively impacting this location's financial viability. I had leverage during this meeting because the economy was poor, businesses were struggling, and workers were being laid off. The unions got the message and started working with each other, management, and reducing unnecessary costs.

On one of my trips to a distribution centers, the general manager confided in me, saying he wasn't happy with his job and the company, we started a discussion about what was best for him. After a couple of talks it was obvious to me that he was in the right position and with a good company. The issue was that he and his boss weren't communicating, and he felt frustrated. I had a talk with his boss to see if I could help them communicate. Unfortunately, the outcome in this case wasn't as successful as before. His boss and the company CEO were upset that I had even had such a discussion with the distribution center manager and they both clearly stated that they were not happy with my actions. I believe that people will do their best work and be happier when there is a good fit in a job and company. I also believed that it was my job as Human Resources Manager to have this type of discussion with employees.

Each of us needs to understand who we are, find out what we do best and hopefully find our purpose and passion. This fellow was in a job and doing okay, but because of his issue with his boss, his heart wasn't in it. This company was not willing to resolve these issues, a mistake.

I've worked with many people who are in the same or similar situations, just going along doing the things other people expect them to do. Granted, family and financial matters need to be met, but my advice is to search for your purpose and passion so you can live your best life.

At Unijax, my overall career choice of being in Human Resources was becoming more a question. Was I in the job I loved? Had I made the right choice out of college? I once thought my function was viewed positively like the work I did at Frito-Lay, but that was the exception. I concluded the function here, and its day-to-day approach wasn't viewed as one that contributed to the company's success. It was viewed my job was to tell line manager "no," "you can't do that," "that's against the law." It didn't have a seat at the big table within the company.

I started to think about career options. I knew it wasn't that I could close my eyes and throw a dart on the wall and hit the correct career from a list of careers, it would take some work on my part. I already was feeling that this career wasn't fulfilling my goals and objectives, and it wouldn't get me to my future vision. I also knew that I had to check my ego during this process, the process I now call my reinvention.

Self-reflection was the next step. I reviewed my core values, strengths, skills, accomplishments, weaknesses, and failures. I also asked acquaintances, friends, and family for their assessment. I put together a table about work and life with the things I liked in the left column and things I didn't like in the right column. After collecting and analyzing the information, the question was, do I want to change, or am I correct in pursuing my current career path? The answer was easy, I needed and wanted to change. With that decision made I had to do a deep dive into how to make this change.

First, I needed to redefine my future vision. What would that future look like? Part of that future was redefining my new self. I had already done lot of the work with self-reflection, and I started picking out those desired work and life items to construct my future vision and self. One of the additional decisions to make was, did I want to work for a company? Or did I want to create my own job? I refined my desired work requirements, work family balance, and lifestyle, and I put together a scoring sheet that defined the details of what I wanted to achieve.

The assessment and reflection process told me what I wanted; it didn't tell me how to achieve those goals. I then started to look for and assess the various reinvention options. I reviewed business trends and market needs. I networked to get information from what I considered knowledgeable people. I also kept challenging myself to get out of my comfort zone. I knew I wanted to stay in the business world, so I then started researching industries, companies, products, and consulting services. I studied the life cycle stage for each and projections of future sales. I applied these to my scoring sheet as well.

During my reinvention options review, I was contacted by a software company regarding a job opening. I researched the company, took two interviews, and applied my scoring sheet. I concluded that going with this company would move me into the growing software world, the sales and consulting world, and open more business disciplines, such as finance and supply chain. It would be working for a company and yet creating my own job.

CHAPTER 9

NEW CAREER

I joined the software company, Management Science America (MSA) which later became Dunn & Bradstreet Software (DBS) and moved back to Atlanta. Their core business was selling and implementing Enterprise Resource Planning (ERP[16]) software systems for business. This was what I was looking for, a change in career path and change was both exciting and scary. I had tons to learn in this new job and industry, During the interview process my future boss explained what the job entailed but I still needed to experience it and internalize what the job was about. It did require high travel, long hours in front of prospects to present and demonstrate the software. The travel and long hours were already a part of my business routine.

My first assignment was as a product representative, the person knowledgeable about the software and its benefits, and to assisting the sales representative with pre-sales activities. That meant I helped to determine the prospective client's needs and show these client's how our systems would fulfill those needs. Orientation and internalization began on day one when I was given several documentation volumes to study and learn every detail of the MSA's software systems. I was also told that soon, a date to be named, I would be tested on the system and all my training—the pressure began.

---

[16] ERP is an integrated suite of business applications such as production, supply chain, accounting, sales, customer service, human resources, and reporting.

The job also included setting the correct expectations about the software and what the prospective client would get. That approach worked well when the client was straight forward in sharing their needs and their goals. But when the clients weren't as forthcoming, the process became complex. For example, if a prospect asked about the software performing a specific task, the answer is yes, because it can do that task straight out of the box or be programmed to do whatever they want. If their question was, does the software do that specific task straight out of the box, the answer would be yes or no depending upon what was already programed into the system. On many occasions the client would ask me to show them how our system processes a specific task. After doing so, the client might say, well, that's not how we do it in our company. The challenge in those cases was to get them to see the potential of revamping their processes because this new software had already incorporated the best business practices. If the client said the demonstrated task would work, then we moved on. The pre-sales dance was a challenge because misleading the prospect will cause credibility and possibly legal problems and at least unhappiness during the implementation and is just wrong.

Most prospective clients hadn't had a new software system in a long time. This evaluation gave them a chance to get the latest and greatest software. Therefore, they wanted every bell and whistle that they could get. They also have been working with processes that are outdated and constrained by their current software. Again, the challenge was to get them to see the potential of revamping their processes. The clients budget limits were another factor in them getting everything they wanted. The approach was to manage the delicate balance between prospective client's expectations, budget, implementation timeframe, and getting them to embrace the new, best business practices. During contract negotiations, when price was the key, clients usually wanted to buy a full software system, but in some cases could only pay for a scaled down version. That meant they could only buy less than what the systems could deliver and probably end up being disappointed.

Once they bought our software, my job was to manage its implementation. All the client's needs, their expectations, and the nice things our systems had to offer were expected. The client's implementation team, who saw the software presentations and demonstrations expected to implement the full software system, which may not have been what their company bought. This required a resetting of expectations.

That disconnect between what was bought and what was expected to be delivered had to be reconciled. The process began with a series of project planning meetings where expectations became real—the client's moment of truth and intense because of the disconnect. I had to establish the reality versus perception and reset the client's expectations. The outcome of these meetings was critical in establishing the success criteria for the implementation project.

When I joined MSA, I was fortunate to go through mandatory training in the software, client's problem identification, networking, handling questions, implementations, presentations, demonstrations, as well as books like *Solution Selling* by Michael T. Bosworth, *Power Base Selling* by Jim Holden. This education was second to none and has benefited me ever since. I remember my final exam which included a presentation to the MSA executives and determined if I had passed to become a product representative. I was full of excitement and eager to demonstrate my new knowledge. I started my presentation and got several hard questions, which I could answer. At one point an executive said, "John, you've sold us, so you can stop now." I started to come back with, "but I've so much more to show you." The executive anticipated what I was thinking, and said, "if you continue on you may un-sell us, so know when to stop." Over time I learned to read my audience and know when enough was enough. I was also fortunate to work with many great people whom I learned from, and a few became lifelong friends, like Mark, Ron, Norma, Ricci, and Keith. I called upon them many times during and after MSA/DBS for help, guidance, and friendship.

One of the valuable lessons I learned during my ten years at MSA/DBS was the whole concept of expectations. MSA/DBS was my first job where I had external clients to satisfy. I've found during my years of managing projects, not just software implementations, for hundreds of clients that the issue of perception versus reality is always present. This was also a factor in my personal life. There were numerous times I promised to be home for dinner, family events, and even an anniversary but I didn't make it because work got in the way. I had set an expectation with my family that I was willing to break by putting my business obligations ahead of them. Each time I put my family last caused hurt, disappointment, and a feeling that I couldn't be trusted to follow through on my commitments to them. That is why my approach to setting, re-setting, and managing promises requires honesty, discipline, patience, follow through, and communication. There are three key points regarding expectations. First, set the correct expectations: understand what other people want and what is achievable. There is a phrase— don't know who said it first, but "under promise and over deliver." Second, when people's expectations are unrealistic, or the situation makes it impossible to meet goals I've had to re-set those expectations to what is achievable. If I hadn't, I would have failed. Third, manage the expectations every day; this is critical because misconceptions and incorrect expectations will creep into the daily routine and become fixed in stone. Once again, failure.

One of the projects I managed while at MSA/DBS was to implement our ERP software for an Agricultural Supply Cooperative. The project seemed to be going well up until the halfway point of the project, measured by our project plan and committed time frame. I had been making regular trips to the clients 'site to stay in touch with the client, get a status report from my project manager, and to be in contact with our consultants onsite.

I would usually fly to the client's location in the early morning, in this case, a Monday, spend the day with my team, meet with the clients to get their opinion and feedback, take the team to dinner that evening, and leave the next morning. This visit schedule was largely dictated by my other numerous projects. On this trip, I sat down with the Project Manager and got my usual update on the project, which included its status, percent of work completed, and percent of budget spent. We also talked about our team's performance, any client issues, and any risk to success. According to the project manager, everything was on schedule, our team was performing well, and there were no client issues.

I then did my walk around, talking to individual project team members. When I was chatting with Mark and Ron, I kept getting the sense something was wrong. I pressed them on how the project was going. After several pointed questions, they finally said, "Well, things aren't going as well as you're being told by the Project Manager." I kept asking questions and got an answer I was horrified to hear. The comments boiled down to the fact that the Project Manager wasn't in control of the project. It wasn't halfway finished, as I had been told, and we had spent seventy-five percent of the budget.

My first reaction was anger. Why had the team members not offered this information earlier? Then I realized that I hadn't been asking straightforward hard questions of them, but instead was being nice and had only asking softball and social questions. I had asked hard questions of the Project Manager but didn't get accurate information. That taught me I can be nice, but I mustn't short cut my responsibility to manage.

My attention turned into finding a solution and developing my action plan. I first went to the Project Manager and asked for the truth. It took a little while, but the Project Manager confessed to our current negative status. The Project Manager's reasoning for telling me everything was okay was that the deficit would be made up before the end of the project. But my experience said the probability of that happening was low and we were in deep trouble. I left the Project Manager's office and went straight to see our client's executive. I wanted to communicate the bad news as soon as I knew it and take responsibility for the problem. I also knew what I needed to do to fix the problem. I met with him and laid out the situation, along with my remedy, which was to replace our project manager, and to go offsite for the balance of that day and the next to recast the project schedule and assignments. I would come back the following day with a report on the recast of the project that would lead to success.

The executive expressed his appreciation for me telling him the news immediately but was upset that we hadn't controlled the project so far. In my mind, I totally agreed with him—I should've done things differently to stay on top of the situation. I had never liked micro managers who got in the way by diving into the smallest detail. But I should've done more of that in this case and adopt the line attributed to President Ronald Reagan, "Trust, But Verify."[17]Reagan used that line several times regard nuclear disarmament discussions with the Soviet Union. The phrase came originally from Suzanne Massie who taught it to Ronald Reagan. Employing that phrase would give me the right balance between getting the information that I needed and micro-managing.

Now, back to how I recast the project. First, I told the current project manager to go to the hotel, pack her bags and fly home. Next, I called the Holiday Inn, where the team stayed, and got a larger room than I had already booked. I also ordered a flip

---

[17] "Trust, but verify." https://en.wikipedia.org/wiki/Trust,_but_verify

chart for my room. I told my team to cancel all meetings the rest of rest of that day and be prepared the meet in my room after lunch with suggestions on how to deliver project success for our client.

We started our meeting that afternoon going over each project task, asking and answering challenging questions about the work completed, the work left to do, and how we were going to get it done within budget and the time frame remaining. We restructured resource assignments and timelines. I kept a flip chart list of other suggested improvements that were incorporated into our plan. At the end the day and a half we had a good plan. We produced a report of the new plan, and I arranged to see the client's executive the next morning.

I met with the executive and presented a plan that would deliver the results with only a two-week delay in completion and would still come in on budget. Instead of significantly going over budget and being two month or more behind schedule. The client wasn't overly happy, but greatly appreciated my candor and our commitment to getting the project done right. My team did deliver the recast project as promised.

I spent the weekend after this incident reformulating my personal project management approach by developing a series of questions and reports, both project-generated and system-generated, that gave me the level of detail I needed. These questions and reports were beyond what we would normally ask and review in our projects. I kept my approach of going on site and talking with each team member to get the answers to new questions. I would continue to have formal reviews of the project, this time with all team members in attendance. This further helped me develop my skills of understanding and communicating executive level information while being able to dive into the details. My lessons on this one were many. First, "Trust but Verify." Second, always to be open and honest with your clients.

Third, deliver bad news early, and fourth, take aggressive action to turn issues around. In other words, get the job done!

The success of a project relies on many factors, but the most important are the people associated with the project. It's vital to know each person's skills, strengths, weaknesses, and agenda. That's easily said, but sometimes hard to determine. The people who have a hidden agenda are the most dangerous. But I've learned that eventually, the hidden agenda will come out, even if sometimes too late.

Another project I was assigned was at a regional medical center who needed a cohesive EPR system with emphasis on inventory control. The problem was that millions of dollars of inventory was being lost each year and their various software systems didn't talk to each other leaving the medical center without a consolidated picture of their organization. The inventory system was PC based which had been in place for some time and loved by the Vice President of Procurement. Shortly after I got the project, we started having reoccurring issues with our software failing to run properly. This wasn't normal because the software had been on the market for years and had hundreds of successful implementations.

The first thing I did was to ask our project team for an assessment. Luckily, Mark was the project manager, and I knew I would get a truthful assessment. "This doesn't make sense and I suggest we bring in our technical experts to evaluate why our software was supposedly failing to run properly" Mark said. I arranged for a technical expert for our company to came in, spend several days running tests and observing daily operations. The assessment was that everything was working as it should. But after he left, the software started to fail again. I then met with the Medical Center CIO to review our findings and asked him, "what's going on?" His answer was uninformative, "I don't know—I guess It's your software." I asked our onsite technical team to keep an eye on failures to see if we could establish a pattern. I then flew back to Atlanta on Thursday with plans to return the following Monday.

The urgency of the problem escalated that weekend when my boss got a call on Saturday morning from the chief surgeon at the Medical Center, saying that he had a gunshot patient on the operating table and couldn't get supplies out of inventory to treat the wound. He said that our system had failed. Of course, my boss went through the roof, called me to ask what was going on and demand I get it fixed. I was horrified that a patient's critical treatment had been impacted.

I flew in on the first flight Monday morning to meet with the Medical Center CIO to sort the software failure out. He was of no help, and just kept saying that we had a software problem. His lack of urgency and ownership in helping to solve the problem was unconscionable. Our technical software team had said to me that our software wasn't the problem and hinted it could be some problem in the Medical Center's IT shop but was not specific. Now I had the client saying it was our fault and my team saying it was the client's fault. Since the CIO was unwilling to help solve the problem, I suggested his IT shop could be causing the failures. He pushed back strongly, and that's when I lost my cool and blasted him about his lack of concern, and for covering for his IT shop ass. My anger resulted in a tongue lashing from my boss but no action on the part of the client to help fix the problem.

The next day, I had a status meeting with the Medical Center CEO, where I gave him the assessment from our technical team and reminding him the software was installed and running well in hundreds of companies. I also told him about my conversation with his CIO. His comeback was to reiterate they were putting in a new inventory control system to stop the loss of millions of dollars each year in inventory. Having a more sophisticated system would help pinpoint the cause of the loss, unlike their current PC based system operated by the inventory department. During our discussion I felt something else was happening which I hadn't been told about, this didn't make sense. I continued to press the CEO but was, once again, given the Medical Center standard answer which was for better inventory control, but my instincts still told me there was some hidden agenda. I once again asked my team to put continuous pressure on the client's project team members with hard questions, diving into an excruciating low level of project detail, and having our technical team babysit every action in IT. I continued to apply heat to the CIO by bringing any little issue or unanswered question to him and demanding resolution. The approach was to keep the pressure and eyes on the client, not accept blame for the software failure issues and hope that someone on the client's team would spill the beans about what was really going on. But no one inside the Hospital would share a reasonable explanation because they either didn't know it or had been told to stay quiet.

Our software system was finally implemented, and the source of the loss was discovered. At my closeout meeting with the Medical Center CEO, he shared that they had suspected foul play with the inventory PC system, and that this was the reason for implement the new software system. I thanked him and realized his plan hinged on hopes of catching the wrong doers. Later, I was told that the Vice President of Procurement, an internal auditor, and a Director in IT, were no longer employed by the Medical Center. The high level of inventory shrinkage was no longer happened with our new system in place. I was also told, through the grapevine, the Director in IT had been crashing our software to discredit it and prevent its implementation.

As if that project wasn't stress enough, Jennifer had graduated from high school, and it was now time for her to go to college. My feeling all along was that this would be a wonderful event for her and the family. Sam was experiencing a normal mom's response to the pending event. As the time approached for her to move out of the house, I started to experience various little physical issue, such as joint pains, acne, and a soreness in my jaw. Once she settled in at school and started taking classes. My physical issues culminated in my jaw locking up, which resulted in me seeing a physician specializing in such matters. His diagnosis was I had TMJ (Temporomandibular Joint Disorders) and suggested various, medications, mouth appliances, and possible surgery, I chose none of these. I wasn't long before the problem went away because my inward stress level had diminished. All along I thought I was fine and was controlling any stress I had, but apparently my inner stress was going crazy. Again, Sam seemed to go through this change well, on the outside, while she might have been churning inside but didn't say so.

In a separate project, again in a regional medical center and implementing the Dunn & Bradstreet ERP software system, I encounter another case of personal agendas, outright deceit, interfering with a project's success. I followed my usual approach by flying to the client's location for status meetings with the project manager and team and the client executives. The project was going along as scheduled with few issues. However, during one of these project review meetings, the CFO complained, "this project is costing more than planned and I want to know why?" His issue was the cost of his project team's travel. He had researched the specific project budget item, and it was out of line. Those were details I wouldn't have had access to reviewing. He further pinpointed the issue; it was because his project people were having to make many trips to our company headquarters in Atlanta. "We haven't had nor are we planning to have any meetings in Atlanta because our meetings were at the Medical Center, where the software was being implemented," I responded. I had found that when I've good people onsite, in this case Norma, and I came in weekly, there was no need for the trips to Atlanta, as everyone was where the work was being done.

I could see the CFO's eyes light up as if he realized the answer to the issue. "I will look into this further." Upon investigation he found that his Project Manager was making personal trips to Atlanta and charging the expenses to our project. Of course, that resulted in that person being let go. I also learned that the client's Project Manager was telling the CFO that our financial software was having problems, which is why there were so many meetings in Atlanta. Of course, there were no software problems, and the software was implemented on time and our company's charges to the project were in line with the plan.

There are several lessons I learned about hidden agendas from these and other situations. First, at the beginning of a project, I started spending more time in depth-dive interviews of all executives associated with the project and all project team members. To understand each person's perspective. Normally the project is handed off to the implementation team with some information about the objectives but rarely in-depth information about the people. My new approach was to begin the interview by asking them to describe what the successful completion of the project would look like and what benefits they will realize. If I get their company's stock answers rather than how they personally will benefit, I'll dig deeper. If they can't visualize and hadn't internalized what project success would look like, I would become concerned and continue to watch their behavior. That, and many more questions, helped me to start to understand their agendas. Watching and listening to people as the project goes along will reveal more about agendas.

I used this technique when I started a project for the U.S. Federal Government in Washington, DC. During my interviews, one project team member told me he was excited because he only had five years until retirement, and this project would take him to that retirement date. When he told me that, and knowing the project was only a one-year project, I knew he would be a major roadblock to success. I met with his boss voiced my concern, he was taken off the project. But there can always be one person who never reveals their agenda, never has a poker tell, and can cause problems. It requires constant monitoring.

Second, I make sure that I'm aligned with the top executives, so that if I've got problems with people on or associated with the project, I can take those issues to the top for resolution. The third is that I drive for results on a project. That means that I just don't offer advice, I push for results and don't cater to hurt feelings. But being tough minded and pushing for results doesn't mean you have to be a horse's backside. My connection to top executives quickly clears up roadblocks and my pushiness moves the project to a successful outcome.

As I noted earlier, setting, re-setting, and managing expectations is one of the keys to success. Two other client situations about expectations come to mind. Our assignment was with food manufacturer to analyze a business issue and come back with recommendations on correcting their problem. I assigned a project manager to go into the client's operation, collect data, analyze, and develop recommendations. I knew this person would do a great job because we had worked together for several years. Time came for our presentation; I flew in to meet with my project manager the evening before our client presentation. At dinner, I reviewed the document being presented. My first reaction was one of surprise and horror. The client had paid several thousand dollars, and I was looking at a document of only a few two-sided pages. To me this didn't pass the weight test, meaning it didn't include enough data, analysis, and options, to back up our recommendations. Our clients expect more than a few pages of summary, regardless of how valid the recommendations may be. It was too late to improve the document since our meeting was at 7 a.m. the next morning. The next day's meeting went as expected, and the client was unhappy with just the summary report. We apologized and committed to produce a thorough document within a couple of days, which we delivered. I believe that all of us think we have a great way of doing or presenting our work. However, the lesson here goes back to the "never assume but verify" rule. Putting yourself in the head of the client is important by asking yourself what their expectations are and do this by asking yourself what you would expect.

Another example was with another regional medical center. The medical center had needed to replace their old business software suite with one that could assist them with effectively managing their operation. The problem was that they didn't have the money to buy and implement the software suites on the market at that time. They went through their evaluation of several systems, selected, negotiation and signed on for our system. Next, they wanted a quote on implementation. They had little money left to spend on implementation, so I could only offer project planning assistance not a full project implementation.

Ricci and I flew to the client's offices for our project kick-off meeting, it became clear that they expected assistance throughout the year-long implementation. They said they had been told this would be the case. We either had a miscommunication within our company, or the client was still negotiating with us. In any case, all I could offer was Ricci, our experienced project manager's help in assisting them with their project planning. If my management wanted to give them additional services, it would have to be their call. My lesson was that I should've been extra clear within my company when client expectations were being set, and I should've had the chance to talk to the prospective client to set their expectations. The second action item may have jeopardized the sale of the software but setting proper expectations will always result in a better sale, a better client, and my company not losing money.

Indeed, expectations go two ways. I must manage the client's expectations of me and manage my expectations of the client. That means I must know the client's company culture and norms. This lesson was reinforced while managing a software implementation in Hollywood for an American Film Production and Distribution Company. Within, the first couple of days of the project, my project manager Ron and I had a meeting with our clients sponsor to present the expense projection. I'm usually asked to estimate the expenses associated with a project, such as airfare, hotels, car rental, meals, and incidentals. In this case when we did, the client reviewed the numbers and then looked at us with a frown on his face. "Will these expenses be sufficient, considering this is Hollywood? I don't want you to come back and ask for more money later," he said. I immediately replied that we were trying to hold down the expenses but would immediately reevaluate the numbers.

Ron and I went back to our work area, looked at each other and smiled. That was the first time I had ever had a client suggest we weren't estimating enough money for expenses. I asked Ron to get prices for high-end Hollywood hotels, vintage car rentals for two cars, not just one, and more expensive restaurants. We tripled the incidental expense amount. We didn't intend to stay at these high-end hotels, rent the expensive vintage cars or eat at the expensive restaurants, but that's what we put into our new estimate. After pricing out a more expensive approach, we went back to get approval. We were asked again if these expenses were sufficient. I said we could make do with these numbers and committed to staying with this budget. Clearly, I hadn't understood the culture of Hollywood studios.

Another misunderstanding of the Hollywood studio culture came when the client sponsor invited our team to attend the weekly director's parties. I agreed that our team could attend and instructed our team that they would conduct themselves as professionally as they would at work. Those of members of our team who wanted to go would be picked up and returned by limousine. At the parties, there were the usual alcoholic beverages, but also plenty of recreational drugs. The beverages and drugs were also available in the limousine. After the first two parties, I stopped our team's participation because a couple of them our team members got out of control. I apologized to our client, and we no longer attended.

CHAPTER 10

THE BIG ONES

D&B Software was in the process of selling the company when I was approached to join IBM. I went through the usual interview process and was offered the position of Global Practice Leader. That position came with two offices, Atlanta, and Warwick, UK because my focus was to work with large multi-national clients.

On my first day with IBM, I reported to my office located at Northside Parkway in Atlanta. I went to the front desk checked in and was told they didn't have me on their list of new employees. I was asked to wait in the lobby until they could sort it out. Thirty minutes later a person from Human Resources approached me to ask me who was my manager, the group I was assigned to and several other questions. The was told to sit tight and he would get thing straightened out. An hour after that he returned to say they were still working on my situation, but he had booked me into an office where I could wait without having to stay in the lobby. I followed him to the booked off where I sat for the next three hours until he returned to give me direction to the cafeteria, so I could get lunch before it closed. After lunch I returned to the temporary office where I stayed until he returned at 4:30 when my handler came to say I was to come back the next morning and everything would be handled. I came back the next day and did get my employee badge made, system sign-on ID and password, and a temporary office. I was also given an instruction manual on their internal mainframe systems which I would be using in my consulting job. However, my laptop wasn't ready and would take a couple of weeks to arrive. I did receive the laptop two weeks later. I can understand how in large corporations 'communication can get messed up, but my first impression of IBM was a bit shaky. A couple of weeks after that my first assignment came and I was to visit a global technologies company, a current client, to see if I could help with a global project.

When I asked the IBM Managing Principal what was expected of me during my visit, I was told that IBM had had two failed attempts to kick-off the in this account. The project was to install Human Resources software in seventy-four sites globally and my assignment was to find a way of convincing them on not throwing us out and turn the project into a success. No pressure in my first assignment. "That sounds like fun," I said, but not really.

The day came and early that morning I flew into the client's North Carolina location and took a cab to the client's office where I met the IBM Managing Principal. We only had a few minutes before we went into our meeting with the client, so we quickly put together our meeting control and coordination plan. What that meant was that the Managing Principal would open the discussion and state the meeting's purpose so that everyone was on the same page. I then would take over for the balance of the meeting until I got the client to a point of agreement or stalemate. I would then turn the control back over to the Managing Principal to recap our meeting, any next steps, and close out the meeting. Our coordination plan included strict adherence to not speaking while your colleague was controlling the meeting. The reason not to jump in is that you would break your colleague's and the meeting's rhythm. Rhythm is important to building the meeting and consensus to a point where agreement is achieved, and your meeting goals are met and therefore a success. This requires trust, I had established some trust with this Managing Principal through our phone conversations but since we hadn't work together it required a leap of faith from both of us.

We were ushered into the meeting room by the receptionist, found our assigned seats at the head of a large U-shaped table. As is customary, we all introduced ourselves. I took the opportunity to give information on my background, qualifications, and previous project successes. What struck me in listening to the client's introductions was that almost everyone at the table was a Chief Information Officer. I thought that was unusual and it seemed unnecessary to have that many CIO's. However, we proceeded, and each CIO told their story of how this IBM project had failed so far. I listened intently because I had to let the client vent, the end of which seemed like hours coming. "So, what are you going to do to make this project a success?" Our main CIO liaison said. I like these kinds of questions because they give me total control of the meeting. I started by getting their permission to ask some questions. Most of the questions were to confirm information that I had in advance. However, as usual I asked a few questions that let me show the value of what we had to deliver.

It took a while, but I had the chance to ask a key question: "Have you conducted a survey of the telecommunications to and from each site and the computer hardware in each site?" I knew from my international experience that not all locations around the world have great telecommunications nor robust computers which causes projects to fail. Each CIO immediately started looking at each other and one finally said, "Well, I'm sure we did," and turned to the CIO in charge of telecommunications and hardware for confirmation. That CIO said, "Well, we really don't have that information." I let that set for a few seconds, and then said that wasn't unusual, but that the new system they were implementing needed a certain level of telecommunications and hardware to work properly. The CIOs started questioning one another as to why no one had thought about that before. Finally, one CIO said, "If we need to do a survey, we don't have the people available to do the job." I remained silent and waited for them to settle down and one asked me if we did that type of work. "Yes, we do, and would be happy to provide an estimate of cost and time frame to complete it" I said. A couple of things had just happened: we had the opportunity to sell more business and an opportunity to do a small project to show we could deliver success. At that point I turned the meeting back over to the Managing Principal who correctly closed the meeting with our assignment to get a proposal back to him quickly. After we left the client, I committed to having that proposal back to the Managing Principal by end of business the next day. I felt very good about the meeting, getting more information about what didn't work helped, but you must listen to the client's needs. This Human Resources project wasn't complex, and it never should've had two failed starts.

As promised, I completed the proposal with the help of Keith, one of my experienced project managers that joined me at IBM from D&B Software and sent the proposal out the next day. Within two weeks our proposal was accepted, and we were off and running to deliver our survey of forty-two of their seventy-four sites in Europe/Middle East, Asia Pacific, and the Americas. The sites not surveyed had telecommunications and hardware upgrades over the past year and should be okay. I asked Keith to be the second in command and the leader of the work in Europe, which he agreed. He and I selected Project Managers from the IBM talent pool for the Asia Pacific and Americas leader roles. The project took two months, we dispatched people to collect the data from twenty of the sites, while we were able to get information by email or phone from the remaining twenty-two sites. Our survey revealed that work needed to be done in thirty-two of the sites. Some of the issues we found were local computers that were being shared, the new system needed a dedicated computer, some computers were too old and needed to be replaced, some needed upgrades, and some sites didn't have the connectivity band width needed. In short, they weren't ready to implement the new software in all seventy-four sites world-wide. The data we collected was invaluable because it showed them exactly what and where work was needed. The client developed their infrastructure upgrade plan, and we rolled it into our implementation plan.

The lessons I learned from this example are: 1) Always verify any information that you have about a project and client; 2) Don't waste time explaining, alibiing, or defending past mistakes. Focus on moving the project and client to a position of success. Let the client vent—that is important—then move them forward; 3) Perform a thorough due diligence on the client's current project readiness; 4) Continue to ask question throughout a project to prevent failures. In this project, the survey provided information about a significant number of locations which couldn't run the new software. Of course, not knowing this would have caused another project failure.

My team and I had passed the first test of collecting data for our client. At that point we were showing success right out of the gate, and we were given the go ahead and launched the discovery phase of original worldwide project by visiting several key global locations to meet with country executives, determine the local and country requirements for the software, and obtain their support for the project. During this initial discovery phase our team each worked on establishing relationships with their client counterparts which improved their sense of confidence in us, but we couldn't stop we had more to do every day to maintain that confidence.

One of our stops during our discovery phase visits was Amsterdam. While we were in their Amsterdam office, the VP of HR and IT Director came to me to say they were concerned and couldn't see how we were going to complete such a complex project on time and on budget. This concern isn't an uncommon one on a perceived complex project, especially when it's divided into three theater implementation teams: Americas, Europe/Middle East, and Asia-Pacific. It's understandable that the number of moving parts might boggle the mind, but I've found that it's easier to understand something if you break it down into smaller pieces. When they voiced their concern, I suggested we go into one of the empty meeting rooms with a white board so I could draw out our approach—Most consultants love to draw on the white boards and I'm no exception. I started to draw a timeline for a single location. I explained the team would first verify that they had a good connection to the server, that computers were equipped as needed, then convert their existing data, load the data into the new system, train one person to enter new data into both systems. After getting the first step completed and signed off, the training team would come in and conduct the balance of the training. The last step was a training person would follow up with each site two weeks later to see if there are any problems or questions. In the meantime, we had training people available by phone or email to help as well. Most sites were small and steps one and two were completed in two weeks. The larger sites the steps were completed in three to four weeks.

I drew out these three steps and time frames on the board, and then showed how each of the teams would go from location to location and repeat the process. That made it clear enough that they understood. I then extrapolated by the number of teams who would be working simultaneously, which gave them the picture of the total timeline to completion. I also built in "open weeks" in case issues came up. I only had to show three teams working simultaneously on the white board to get complete understanding and agreement with the approach. The approach worked as planned and we did have to use some of the open weeks for issues, but in the end, the project was successful, and was on time and on budget. It did help that of their seventy-four locations twenty-two were smaller, and their individual complexities were minimal. This method of breaking complex projects/tasks down into smaller pieces has worked well for me. I not only get more comfortable with the project at hand, but so do the people I work with—a valuable approach for me in business and in my day-to-day life.

The balance of the project, after discovery was approved. I assumed the role of Engagement Manager and ran the Project Management Office, PMO. The role of the PMO is to be the key customer interface, oversee the IBM resources, track the project's progress, track billings, quality control, track adherence against the methodology, and handle other project administrative duties.

With the PMO in place, I started to get reports on the weekly hours worked, the expenses being charged against the project, and other vital information. The objective was to stay on track with all items and to know, in advance, the amount of a client's monthly invoice. When I received invoices from our IBM billing system, I reconciled them against the advanced reports out of the PMO. I preferred to personally check each invoice and present the invoices to my clients. That way I could answer any questions they may have rather, than the invoice just showing up in an email. My approach usually gets the payment processed quicker.

In this case the invoices were several months late, the client's IT Director had been asking for the invoices because they wanted to pay them within the correct budget period so they could stay on track. I had also been calling my IBM project billing office asking for the invoices, without results. I finally received the first monthly invoice, checked it, and discovered the numbers were severely off and didn't match the PMO report. Since the client's IT Director was anxious to get the first invoice, I told him that the numbers needed further checking and I would do that within a couple of days. I called our project billing representative at the IBM project billing office in New Jersey and insisted we reconcile this first invoice on the phone. We were on the phone for over an hour and couldn't reconcile the numbers. I became frustrated and asked to speak to his manager. That conversation was equally nonproductive. The manager told me to just give the client the invoice and things would even up later. I told the IBM Billing Manager that I wouldn't and would only present an invoice that could be reconciled. I requested he work with his employee to send me a correct invoice and I needed it immediately. His response was he would investigate it. I took this approach because a mentor I had early in my career told me to take care of the client first. He also said not to blindly do what your company wanted done if it didn't make sense, so I followed his advice. What that meant was that I had to go back to my client and tell him the invoice would be a few days later than I thought. Not a good impression to make with a client where IBM had had past problems.

After two days, I call the New Jersey billing office to find out they were still having trouble producing a revised invoice. The billing representative said he was working on the invoice, but it was complex, and it would take several more days. I told him I was confused since the information our team had entered in the IBM system was straight forward and not complex. All he needed to do was process an invoice for that billing period. Once again, I was frustrated and called his manager to inform him that nothing had been resolved. My next step was to escalate the issue to the director level in the billing organization, who promised to get the matter resolved.

The next day the billing representative called me to ask permission to visit my client's accounting office in New Jersey to help resolve the invoices. That didn't make much sense, but he wanted to see our weekly PMO reports we sent to the client which aids in the client's accounting function to reconcile our invoices. I reminded our representative that I had sent him our weekly PMO reports when this issue first came up. However, I okayed him going. This whole experience seemed like an episode from the 1960s TV show, *The Twilight Zone.*

Now I was receiving emails from an IBM vice president telling me to collect money from the client, immediately! I sent an email back saying that I wouldn't present an incorrect invoice. I also said that I would create correct invoices myself, on site, to present to my client since I couldn't get an accurate one from the IBM New Jersey Billing Office. Creating your own invoices isn't permitted at IBM and I was going way out on a limb. I did create several invoices that matched our monthly PMO reports, and presented them to my client's IT Director, who approved them for payment.

I waited a few days and called the IBM billing director to see where he was in his investigation and invoice cleanup process. He explained that our billing representative had visited the client's account office in Florida and was working to clean up the invoices. I immediately said, "Florida?" He confirmed Florida. I explained that I had only authorized the representative to go to the client's New Jersey office. They only processed these invoices in New Jersey, not in Florida. Which I had clearly explained to the billing representative. The IBM billing director said he would call me back in an hour. An hour later, he called to tell me that another billing representative would be handling my project. I informed the director that I would continue to create local invoices and send his office a copy until I received one from his office that could be reconciled. I sent an email to the IBM Vice President, stating the same thing I had just told the IBM billing director and added that I was at least collecting money for IBM.

With the issue handled and our consistent good work on the project the client jokingly issued a challenge regarding project success, more specifically coming in on time and on budget. It seems that project failure was more usual than not in their past. I answered in kind, hoping they would go along by saying that if we came in on time and on budget, I would like for the IBM client team and our project team to be given a dinner party at the client's expense. The client immediately agreed, but asked, "Where should we have it?" I suggested we have a closeout meeting in our Paris office and then a dinner party afterwards. It was agreed and communicated to all project members.

We finished the project on time and on budget, and now Paris. Not all the project team members could attend because some of them were moving on to other projects with date conflicts. The week after the project ended, we met in the IBM Paris office for our closeout meeting. I characterize the closeout meeting as ideal with honest give and take discussion on what worked and what didn't work during the project. The conclusion was the client was happy. My European Project Manager made dinner reservations for twelve at Le Grand Café Capucines, near the Opera National De Paris, where we met later that evening for a fantastic meal which began with nonstop wine, several seafood towers, followed by individual meal orders. Before the evening was over there was desert and coffee all around. The next day the client's personnel wanted to take the opportunity to sight see in Paris. My team, however, had business in our office and couldn't join them. We met up with a couple of people from both project teams still in Paris again for dinner that last evening in Paris before we all flew out to various parts of the world.

That evening we went to a restaurant, specializing in Duck a l'Orange, and had an interesting history. The front door was a Dutch door where the top or bottom can open individually, or both can open with the closing a latch. The story goes that the restaurant owner wanted to decide who was allowed in the restaurant and would only open the top when there was a knock on the door. He would then decide if the person knocking would be admitted. Which is what we did to gain entrance. This came in handy during WWII when Paris was occupied by the German Army and his restaurant was officially closed. The owner would only admit a select clientele such as the staff of an underground newspaper close by so the workers could eat. The owner's approach to making his l'Orange was by filling jars, like Mason jars, with his own concoction of oranges, sugar, water, and his other ingredients. He cured the ingredients by placing them on a shelf that encircled the restaurant near the ceiling. He would take down the jars at the end of the line each day when its contents were ready for serving. He and his staff then moved each jar around the circle to fill the empty space. We quickly discovered he was a colorful fellow who enjoyed entertaining his guest by telling stories and singing. The stories and singing became more robust and animated as the wine flowed and the evening progressed. This made for a fun evening and a place to return. I only wish I could remember the name of the restaurant, but there was probably too much wine and fun on my part.

At this point in my career, I had accumulated several million miles on Delta, British Air, and Lufthansa. Returning home after one of my long trips to Asia, I was exhausted. That evening, I landed back in Atlanta, drove the hour to my home, dropped my bags and immediately went to dinner with Sam. She drove, because I was exhausted and even fell asleep in the car on the way to the restaurant. The next morning, I took rolls of film to the local lab for developing. I approached the counter, and the clerk asked me a question, but I didn't understand what was being asked. "Excuse me can you repeat that?" I asked. The clerk did and I still couldn't understand the language being used. I asked for clarity again, and still couldn't understand. I finally pointed to the developing option I wanted on a laminated counter card used to help customers make decisions, just like I sometimes had to do in China when ordering food. After leaving the store I realized that after several weeks of listening to various accents speaking English, I couldn't understand this southern United States accent (my ears weren't used to it). But before that day had finished, I was back understanding what people were saying.

The lesson I learned in this situation was that my mentor's advice, to always put your client first and develop a good business relationship, were true. Don't always do exactly what your company wants you to do if it jeopardizes a good client relationship. I say that because our project and team got high praises from this client, and additional business came to IBM. The second thing was my dislike for bureaucracy, which in this case was reinforced.

In 1996 while still at IBM our family built a house in Woodstock, GA. I was a three-story house with a full in-law apartment in the bottom level where the bedroom and bath areas were underground and the other rooms such as living room and kitchen had windows to the outside yard. The reason for building this large of a house was that my mom and dad weren't in good health, they lived in Florida, and I wanted them closer. After Sam and I talking it over we agreed to build the new house and ask my parents to move in with us.

I eventually left IBM and became a Partner at KPMG Consulting specializing on global practice development. I was new to the company when I got the assignment to implement Payroll and Human Resources systems at a global financial company offering wealth management, investment banking and financial services, located in Switzerland. This implementation was a part of a larger Enterprise Resource Planning (ERP) implementation that included Financial, Human Resources and Payroll. One of my North American Partners had the financials; I had Human Resources and Payroll. The Managing Partner on the engagement was from the London, England, office.

I began recruiting Norma and Keith, former colleagues from IBM and MSA/D&B and interviewed the project team candidates that I didn't know. I wanted to see if the new candidates were qualified and fully understood what it meant to work on an international project and be away from home for up to a year. The first half of the interview was about what I would expect from them, their skills and experience. The second half was what they could expect from the assignment, including how living in another country can be fun, but it isn't the same as home. I selected my project team mainly from seasoned U.S. consultants and combined them with a contingent of newer consultants from our German office, some of whom are still friends today.

Next, I arranged for my first meeting with the client in Switzerland and took my two senior consultants with me. I suggested to my team that we meet in Switzerland the day before our meeting and book into the Marriott Hotel. The time came, and I flew out of Atlanta and arrived at the airport the next morning. The airport was only a fifteen-minute ride to the hotel, but I enjoyed every minute. That was the first time I had been in Switzerland and the scenery was beautiful, the taxi was a late model Audi, the driver was a great conversationalist and knowledgeable about many subjects, including our project city. We arrived at the Marriott, which is located across a river and up the hill from the city central. Incidentally, the river opens into a nearby lake. Another plus is that the client's office was about eight minutes 'walk from our hotel. I usually preferred to stay in hotels native to that country instead of American-centric hotels, but this hotel was convenient, had good food, and a great view. The hotel was a typical Marriott look and feel, with a bar and American café but one exception; a Thai restaurant, the White Elephant, was connected to the hotel, a restaurant I would have to explore. I met my team in the bar before dinner to go over the agenda for the next day. Our plan was to meet with the client that next day and start getting acclimated to the city. I wanted to have the details worked out so that when the balance of the project team came in two weeks later the project could immediately start.

After work on that first day, my colleagues and I met in the bar for an after-work drink before going to eat in the White Elephant restaurant. Upon entering the spicy aroma was welcoming and I was excited to explore what was on the menu. I ordered a chicken curry dish and was asked how hot I wanted it. They had a rating scale of heat of 1, 2, or 3 elephants. I was a wimp and only got a number 2, which I did over the next year as I'd ordered almost every dish they made, but only once did I order a number 3. It was good but too hot for me.

Two weeks later, everyone was assembled in Switzerland, and the project kick off. Our day-to-day client representative was the Human Resources/Payroll department, and they had hired a third-party consultant to advise them on the implementation as well. This was something that didn't make sense at first. I later learned that there was zero trust between this department, corporate management, and the Information Technology (IT) department. Since we were hired by corporate and IT, I finally understood; the Human Resources/Payroll management wanted their "own" consultant. In any case, we kicked off the project, and started doing the work. One issue I had was that we weren't allowed to meet with the Human Resources/Payroll management without the Third-Party Consultant controlling the meeting. I brought this issue up more than once with our KPMG Managing Partner and was told not to make waves. That was against every basic principle in consulting and was on the list of "Why Projects Fail." We must have direct access to the client and their executives to clear roadblocks, to not let the project stall, and deliver the expected success. But, even with this impediment, we made progress and expected to meet our deliverables on time and on budget.

Within a couple of weeks one of my U.S. consultants, a new team member, started to complain about how hard it was to be deprived of things she was used to back home. When she was selected, she had asked if her husband could accompany her so they could be together in Switzerland, and her request was approved. Apartments had been arranged for the full-time consultants, so to have her husband with her wasn't a problem. He had to pay for his trip and her chargeable expenses weren't increased for him. Her requests increased and turned to complaints and now she wanted a car to be provided for her husband because he was bored and wanted to travel. I reminded her this wasn't in the budget and this assignment wasn't a vacation. Switzerland had plenty of transportation options he could use. After I rejected her demands, she went to the KPMG Managing Partner. I, of course, was asked to meet with them both to review her demand. I set up the meeting and let her go through her complaints until she said that she hadn't been told what to expect on this assignment. That's when I stopped the conversation and reminded her of our lengthy conversations about what life would be like on this assignment. Her comeback was that she needed the things she requested to make this assignment work for her. I then repeated her statement back to her: "So if your husband doesn't get a car, for example, this isn't going to work for you, correct?" She said it wouldn't work. At that point I told her to pack her bags and leave on the next day's plane for home, she was off the project. Her face said she was in shock. She apparently had assumed she would get what she wanted. She got up and left the room.

The Managing Partners looked at me and asked if we could've worked something out, and I said *No*, because she's constantly complaining, and her performance is lacking. She will destroy the team if she prevails with her demands. So, she's off the project, period. When I made the announcement to the project team, I was given handshakes and thanks. We all went to dinner together that night at an excellent restaurant on the banks of the lake to celebrate.

In my life, I've had to move many times, and I had to adapt to that new place. I'm thankful that I learned the art of adaptation. I do get angry when people, especially Americans, who refuse to adapt and take a potentially extraordinary experience and not appreciate it.

The project continued, except the pace of output increased once the dead-weight person had left. At that point we were about a month away from completion. One day I got a message that I was to travel across town to another office for a meeting. No word on what the meeting was about, who would be present, or what we, KPMG, wanted to accomplish. I was starting to get the definite feeling that our Managing Partner didn't possess any intestinal fortitude.

I ordered a taxi and traveled to the meeting site. Upon walking into the meeting room, I saw my managing partner, the partner on the Financials sitting on one side of the table and no one on the other side. I took a seat, leaned over to the KPMG Partner, and asked, "What's this all about?" The reply was that we were going to meet the new Chief Information Officer. My instincts had been on high alert since the moment I got the message to go to the meeting, and this information only reinforced my feelings that we were in for a battle.

It was at least ten minutes later when the new CIO and his entourage came in and sat on the opposite side of the table. He proceeded to establish, in his own mind, that he oversaw our ERP implementations and that he was in the only person in total control. He also stated that if we didn't cooperate fully, we would be kicked out. Since I had lived in Germany and traveled to Germany on many occasions, I knew immediately that he was German and not Swiss. My conclusion was confirmed when he kept turning to "his guys" and speaking in German, not Swiss German. His arrogance was such he didn't think any of these Americans at the table could possibly understand what he was saying.

After his initial salvo, he turned this attention to me. It seems that the Human Resources/Payroll project wasn't yet under his total control, and he wanted my commitment to him and only to take orders from him and his guys, and not the Human Resources/Payroll management. This was a demand that I wouldn't give into, which made him more animated and brought nudges from my fellow partners to shut up and agree. I continued to be polite and spoke softly in my American accent, stating again that I couldn't comply, since I reported to the Human Resources/Payroll department management. Then the new CIO asked that I do an assessment of the resources needed to implement Payroll to which I replied that I would see if that was possible.

The new CIO finally gave up and turned to my KPMG Managing Partner and said they would discuss this one-on-one. At that point, the CIO adjourned the meeting. As a side note, the new CIO and his team smoked one cigarette after another during the closed-door meeting. This was a pressure tactic, knowing that most Americans didn't smoke. I was starting to turn green but wouldn't give into his demands.

The new CIO stood at the meeting room door to shake our hands as we left. When he shook my hand, I replied to his goodbye in German. He was startled and asked if I spoke German to which I replied in German that I did. He wanted to talk more but given the poor reception and off-putting side bar comments to his guys, I chose not to give him the time and let his egocentric language assumption leave him wondering. The meeting encounter simply solidified my feeling that my managing partner was a Neville Chamberlain type, go along to get along.

A couple of weeks later, my managing partner pressed me for my assessment on the resources needed to implement the payroll system since we were coming to the end of the Human Resources phase of the project. I complied only to have the Human Resources/Payroll management blow their stacks the following week at my having shared information with the new CIO. I knew that my action would probably bring on problems for me. I could either do it and risk the ire of the Human Resources/Payroll management, or not do it and risk the anger of my real management. Anyway, since I resisted playing ball with the new CIO, I figured that I was out of the project. Interestingly, we finished the Human Resources phase, but the payroll phase didn't get funding to move forward. I suspect, because of the new CIO's tyrannical approach, and he and his team's tenure with the client was short lived.

The lessons learned in this story are: 1) never take a project where you don't have direct access to the executive decision makers and 2) never assume and prejudge anyone—it will only create issues for you.

After several projects at KPMG, the company split the audit and consulting practices, with the consulting portion went public, and I decided to leave. I had had an opportunity to sign a contract, to stay with the company, which would have locked me into this company and limit the future places I could work. The carrot was that signing meant potentially a lot of money in stock that would pay off in the future. But my instincts said staying wouldn't be the right move for me and it was time to branch out on my own.

III

INDEPENDENCE

CHAPTER 11

TRANSITION STRUGGLE

During my exit from KPMG, I had talked to Mark and Keith about launching a start-up company to sell and deliver the work we had been doing for years. We all had consulting experience and contacts that would help kick-off a new company, and we no longer had any non-compete issues. After several discussions, in March of 2000 we formed a company, Navado, Inc., to sell and deliver consulting services. However, we also wanted to do something different, and after a lot of research and brainstorming, we chose to add Business Applications Services to our portfolio, what is now known as Software as a Service (SaaS). The concept is that companies rent the software rather than buy it. We approached several of the leading software companies and were told they weren't interest. Their current model was to sell the software, charge for implementation services, and charge for ongoing software maintenance. Their attitude was that their model was lucrative, so why change it? What these software companies weren't seeing is the customer trend to get away from this expensive model to a more creative and less costly approach, while at KPMG selling software implementation services to clients outside of the US was increasingly more difficult because of cost. Those prospects and clients were the forerunners of the trend.

During my discussions with PeopleSoft, about our new idea, I was offered the rights to sell and implement PeopleSoft in Ireland. I grabbed the chance and began searching for an Irish business partner who would have more detail knowledge about the market along with the contacts. After working with my international contacts, a couple of trips to Ireland and several lunches, dinners, and drinks at pubs I found a good partner. We sorted out the agreement, legalities, and launched our initiative. Spring boarding on that idea that the market demanded lower cost solutions, we sought out and got the rights to be a reseller and implementer of Great Plains software, which later became Microsoft Dynamics. Navado continued to sell consulting services, and with the two software offerings, we had three product lines.

We also had several ongoing consulting contracts on our own, and we worked with larger consulting companies to augment their staff. However, selling Great Plains and PeopleSoft didn't go as planned. Great Plains wasn't well known and needed a couple of years to develop a good market and PeopleSoft still was too expensive for the Irish market.

I self-funded the start-up of the company with the idea of getting outside investors as we increased our revenues. But the time and money needed to build the business didn't match the revenues coming in and we didn't have investors after making numerous pitches. I didn't have the capital to continue funding the company so after much discussion we decided to shut down the business. I paid off all our debts and money owed to employees and partners and closed the doors. My regret is that I talked several friends into following my idea, only to fail.

The lessons I learned were that each one of our product lines would have taken a concentrated effort to succeed, and we didn't have enough time, money, or staff resources. In summary, we spread ourselves too thin and were underfunded. Mark and Keith went off on their own to do independent consulting.

I was still living in the three-story house we built in 1996. It was good to have been in one house for four years, it was grounding. I didn't know immediately what I wanted to do, so I decided to take three months to sort it out. Jennifer had graduated from college with a degree in education and was working in a county school teaching first grade. Sam was continuing to work in her career as the Registered Nurse.

I realized that I could do just about anything I wanted, so it was a good time for another reinvention. I followed the same method I'd used before, and I started my second reinvention with self-reflection. That meant I had to check my ego and figure out who I was—something I'm continually working on. A lot had happened over the years including gaining knowledge and learning lessons. I did a deep dive into defining my core values and assessing my strengths, skills, and accomplishments. I asked others to describe me along those lines as well. I wrote down the work I like to do and what I didn't like to do. Part of the reflection was answering the question about creating my own job or working for a company. Lastly, I defined my vision of my future life. I didn't define a specific job, that would come after three more reinvention steps.

Next, I reviewed business trends and market needs. I networked to get information from people I considered knowledgeable. I also kept challenging myself to get out of my comfort zone when seeking and analyzing the information gathered. I knew I wanted to stay in the business world, so I started researching industries, companies, products, and consulting services. I studied the life cycle stage for each, and projections of future sales.

After my self-reflection, business review and research, I was ready to take the next step and decide. I chose, with great enthusiasm, to enter the world of Business Process Outsourcing Consulting (BPO). That industry was at the beginning of the life cycle curve, with billions of projected sales in the future. I knew potential clients would be looking for knowledge, experience, and a logical approach to help them. I started with increasing my knowledge by reading everything I could find on BPO to gain a foundation. I developed a list of countries, including the US, where work might be outsourced. There were a few countries already doing outsourcing work, which gave me a starter list. I developed a ten-factor scoring system to evaluate each country and placed them into one of three markets: Established (where outsourcing had been going—mainly manufacturing), Prime (where outsourcing was going now), or Emerging Market (where outsourcing was projected to go). I also spent a couple of weeks in Washington, D.C. to visit embassies and discuss their countries 'plans or receptiveness regarding outsourcing.

Within each market, I researched the outsourcing companies providing BPO services and collected detailed information about their services and where possible got the names of their clients. It wasn't always possible to get client names since many of them wanted to be kept anonymous.

This research and analysis resulted in developing an entire outsourcing program – the methodology: where to go, who to go with, how to be successful, risks, and the step-by-step project plan. I also developed sales materials and set out to pitch my services. This was the official establishment of my consulting company, J. Phillip Partners (JPP). Coming up with a name for a new company is a chore. I wanted the name to sound strong, established, and trustworthy. I also didn't want to pay anyone to come up with a name. I knew of companies who paid large sums to have names developed. I chose to use my first initial, middle name, and the word partners. The partners part of the name signifies that I would bring in other consultants, such as Mark, Ron, Norma, Keith, and Ricci, as needed and if they were available, on assignments. It sounded good to me, and better yet the name was free. I also chose as my logo colors a medium blue, because I knew from my IBM days that blue was a color of trust.

During my start-up phase, I was approached to take a position as Eastern Region VP of Sales for Covansys. Covansys was a company that had sold staff augmentation from its beginning, but after being bought by a private equity company they were moving to a traditional IBM type consulting approach.

I took what I considered to be a temporary position, while still worked on selling my consulting services. During my three months of contemplation, I had learned that I didn't want to work for a corporation but needed to be on my own. However, one does have to pay the bills in the interim.

At Covansys, I quickly discovered an internal political battle was going on between the original owner and the private equity company. The original owner didn't think changing the current model was wise since the old model had worked for many years, but the Private Equity company wanted to evolve to what they considered higher level consulting work. That led to a division in the company between those who had been with the company and the original owner, and those recently hired to transform it. The impact on the sales function was that we had two sales groups. The official one, which I managed for the Eastern Region, and a shadow sales group that continued to call on customers to sell staff augmentation. It was confusing for clients and potential clients when they would get calls from both groups. Indeed, we were working against ourselves.

Despite the issues, I continued to build the new sales team. On one business trip to New York to recruit sales representatives I came face to face with a life changing event. That event inspired me to write my story I call *Sky of Dust*.

It was a crisp September morning[18], just another day, and I was in my room recovering from the night before with my team

---

[18] September 11, 2001

for dinner and drinks. My mouth felt, tasted, and smelled like old tennis shoes. I got up, found the bathroom, showered, shaved, and drank a Coca Cola to get me going to do the job I was there to do. We were interviewing sales candidates at the Marriott Marque in Times Square, and the first interview was to be at 7:30 for breakfast. The day was scheduled to go long with back-to-back interviews. I got to the restaurant early so I could eat and recover. Just as I was starting to feel human again, I was joined by our company's recruiter and the first candidate arrived—a smart young women who seemed to have promise as a sales representative. We finished the interview, shook hands, and told her we would call her the next week. "That would be great and now I'm going to meet a friend who works in the World Trade Center" she said.

As I looked over the next candidate's resume, I got a call from our manager in New Jersey, saying that something was wrong in New York, no specific information was available, but we should leave the city. We didn't of course we were too focused on the interviews. When our second interview didn't show up, we started to hear a buzz in the hotel lobby. "Was it an accident?"…"How many people were hurt?"…"Should we leave the hotel?"…"Should we leave the city?"…"What should we do next?"

Hearing the chatter, the recruiter and I decided to go to my room and turn on the TV. The news was shocking, one plane had hit the World Trade Center, and eight planes were missing with no communications. My adrenaline was pumping, and my instincts kicked in as I evaluated the situation. One plane hitting a building could be an accident, but with eight planes missing in flight, I assumed we were under attack. The question was what to do next. It was just then that we saw the second plane hit the World Trade Center. My colleague was pacing around the room, "I am worried our building will be hit," he said. I tried to calm him by explaining in a logical manner that it wasn't likely, since the buildings around us were taller. Being a yoga instructor and a spiritually sensitive person, he was visibly shaken. "I can feel many souls leaving the earth and I need to get out of this building" he exclaimed. I tried to calm him again by suggesting we change clothes and head south to see if we could help. I knew that I needed to go south, knowing it was a naive thing to do, I would probably be turned away, but I couldn't live with sitting around and not trying to do something.

We changed out of our suits, left the building, and headed south. I could hear military jets flying over us as we left the hotel. My thought was it was about damn time we had air cover.

As my colleague and I headed south against a steady stream of expressionless dust covered people walking north. They stared straight ahead, putting one foot in front of the other. I could hear randomly dispersed coughing among them, something I would experience for several months to come. As expected, we only got about six blocks when the police stopped us. We turned and headed back to the hotel, a young lady hurrying south stopped us to ask what was going on. We told her that two planes had crashed into the World Trade Center, and it appeared the United States was under attack. That information hit her hard, she seemed dazed. Her determination to get to some appointment left her and without saying anything, she turned around and began walking north with the rest of us. She became another in the long line of people walking north with a thousand-yard stare.

When we got back to the hotel, Times Square was a ghost town with papers blowing in the streets. There were no cars except for a limousine that had its door open with the radio on and people were gathered around listening to news reports. It seemed like a scene out of the movie, *The Day the World Stood Still.*

The hotel was setting up security at the entrance, so we decided to walk around for a while. I looked across the street at the NASDAQ building and saw that a construction crew had unrolled a homemade banner with "God Bless America" painted on it. My heart rate quickened, and I felt tears welling in my eyes at the sight of this patriotic banner blowing in the breeze. As we walked the streets, we saw vendors selling freshly made t-shirts of the World Trade Center, the date and "God Bless America" printed on them. Many shops and delis were opening, people started to appear on the streets.

We finally made it back to the hotel and had to go through a rigorous screening process to get back inside. Once there, my colleague suggested we could get out of the city by using his car. I questioned him because the news said all the bridges were closed to vehicles, with no way out of the city. We had seen the thousands of people walking across the Brooklyn bridge, trying to get home. He insisted he knew a way out and could get us to our office in Providence, Rhode Island. I finally agreed to give his idea a try. We packed, ordered his car, and set out on West 45th street toward the Hudson River. We turned right on the Henry Hudson Parkway at the Intrepid Sea, Air and Space Museum, and went North. Soon we were climbing out of the city and as I turned around, I could see the smoke rising from the World Trade Center. A chill ran through me for the first time. I was shaken, my "take charge and keep cool" persona was rocked. I remember saying to my colleague, "The United States will never be the same again, and neither will we."

We worked our way over to I-95 as we headed to Providence. We passed one Army truck after another loaded with troops heading South to the city. Every exit had a police car sitting and observing the few cars that were traveling. It felt as though we were under martial law. All our concerns drove us not to stop until we got to Providence; we had to get to a safe, familiar place.

Once in Providence I checked into the Marriott, called my family, and tried to relax. I couldn't, of course, and stayed glued to the TV. That's when I learned of the Pennsylvania plane down, the Pentagon hit, and the chaos that was griping the nation. My mind confirmed we were under attack, maybe not an all-out invasion, but an attack. I felt helpless to do anything and knew I would be changed forever. Later that night I went to the hotel restaurant for a bourbon and steak dinner, with wine. It seemed like the right thing to do because it gave me comfort and allowed me to escape for a while. I was buzzed enough to sleep, which felt good.

The next morning, I went into the office and tried to schedule a flight home, but I was told that it would be at least Saturday before I could get one. I tried to conduct business but had little motivation. I called my colleague, who was with me in New York, in his office about 11 a.m. to ask him how he was doing; he said he too was having trouble working. That his heart wasn't in it. I decided to leave the office at lunch that day and go back to the hotel. That is something I wouldn't have normally done but I just couldn't work.

The following day I again tried to work but I sat at my desk and couldn't. I noticed that I had developed a cough; my colleague told me he had the same problem (my cough stayed around for a few months).

For the rest of the week, it was still difficult for me to work but my coworkers, who hadn't been in New York City that day, seemed to carry on business as usual. Their usual business demands seemed irritating and selfish to me, and I couldn't engage. I just did idle things and escaped to my hotel as early as I could each day. On Saturday I went to the airport, waited forever and finally got booked on a flight to Atlanta. The airport ticket desk was a zoo, and everyone's nerves were frazzled, including mine. I proceeded to the security screening area which now contained several military personnel with automatic rifles at the ready. A sight that I would see many times over the coming months. I arrived at the boarding gate and tried to settle in as I had done thousands of times, but I kept scanning the room looking at everyone's face. I noticed a couple of Middle Eastern-looking men and I found that I couldn't take my eyes off them. There was no evidence of anything wrong, but I started to formulate a plan in case trouble started. I also noticed that many others in the lounge were staring at them as well. After we boarded, I took notice of where they sat and revisited my plan for trouble. Since I was sitting on the aisle and they were behind me, my plan was to block them in the aisle and hope other passengers joined in. My plan probably would've never worked, but it gave me comfort to have a plan.

Nothing happened and I arrived safely back in Atlanta. As is the custom in business, nothing stops for more than a day, so I was on a plane again that next week.

As time passed, I still couldn't get motivated and found the old rah-rah of "let's do this for the team" hollow and without importance. Events like that day put everything in perspective.

The thought of delayed air cover stayed with me and years, after things settled down and the events were better documented, I researched the military air response to 9/11. My research revealed that there were slight time frame differences by a minute or two, depending upon who was telling the story. But the most recognized and comprehensive account of these events would be Lynn Spencer's book Touching History.

My summation is that during the time of 9/11, our air defenses were focused on threats coming from outside the Continental United States (CONUS) rather than any threat from inside. There were protocols and training in place for hijacked planes but not for suicide hijackings. The CONUS alert fighter coverage on 9/11 totaled only five percent of those on alert at the height of the Cold War. There were only 4 alert fighters in the

Northeast corridor, east of the Mississippi River and north of the Mason Dixon line. There was, of course, additional coverage assigned to the President and based in DC.

The first suspicion of a problem was at 8:15 a.m. when American Airlines 11 didn't respond to Boston Center's instructions to ascend in altitude. A series of overheard radio transmission from AA 11 and its veering off course prompted the Boston Center to contact FAA Command Center, and then at 8:34 a.m. called Otis Air National Guard (NEADS, Northeast Air Defense Sector) to scramble the alert fighters. At 8:46 a.m. two F-15s from the 102 Fighter Wing were scrambled, and at 8:53 a.m. they were airborne. At 8:47 a.m. American Airlines 11 hit North Tower of the World Trade Center. The alert fighters arrived in the Atlantic off New York City at 9:03 a.m. and are instructed to maintain a holding pattern. There seemed to be some confusion over a course of action. It wasn't until 9:13 a.m. that these two fighters left their Whiskey 105 holding position, offshore from ground zero to establish a Combat Air Patrol (CAP) over New York City.

After doing my research, my question was answered. The military was committed to performing their jobs and losing their lives if necessary. The problem was that our security preparedness didn't have procedures in place to handle this type of threat, so it took time to work through what action to take. It's my understand that procedures have been updated after 9/11 so that these types of threats can be dealt with quickly and by established procedures.

On my first visit back to the New York City, the circumstances didn't allow for a visit to Time Square or the Trade Center area. I will go back someday because that was the place where my life changed.

The key event that told me it was time to leave Covansys and get back to my dream for J Phillip Partners was when I was pursuing an outsourcing deal with a global conglomerate. I had made it through all the sales hurdles and was looking forward to visiting our outsourcing facility in India with the prospect. I had set up the trip, and made my reservations, and felt the trip would win us the business. Two days before I was to leave for India, I received a call from my boss saying I wasn't going, the visit would be handled by the local management in India. I had made many sales trips to India before and knew local management couldn't replace the relationship I had built with this prospective client. I was furious and told my boss so, who replied that the decision was made, and I needed to forget it.

That attitude told me something else was going on and I continued to investigate. It took a few days before I learned the real reason for my not going. The original owner wasn't in favor of us selling to this global company because he felt they were a competitor and were using this sales opportunity to steal information, especially during the India site visit. The global prospect had an external consultant helping them with their selection process and with whom I had established a good relationship. I learned from him that the India trip was a disaster, and that, me not being there had cost us the business. My job became more and more difficult, and my commitment less and less. There was an internal political struggle at Covansys where the new direction was being questioned. A growing consensus was to go back to selling staff augmentation and not the IBM model of consulting which required more resources and expense. These events, and those of 9/11 told me it was time to leave the company and as events unfolded, I was asked to leave—I wholehearted agreed.

My lesson with Covansys was to listen to my gut and stay with my plan, and my core values. Listening to my gut when I saw chaos in the company and if I couldn't affect a change, leave. Stay with my plan to be on my own by working harder to bring in the sales so I could launch J Phillip Partners. Always stick with my core values and not "go along to get along".

CHAPTER 12

FINDING A NICHE

My company was ready to go to market. Now I could get back to my first love of being on my own and execute my plan. I started networking like crazy to sell my consulting services. I sought out and attended every business association, social, and community event I could find. My approach and pitch were the same with slight changes given the specific event. I met as many people as I could with a handshake, smile, and my five second introduction. If I got questions, I would follow up with a thirty second expanded pitch and answer the questions. I also handed out business cards at the end of the conversation. As part of my launch preparation, I developed a five and thirty second pitch and a three-minute pitch. If I was pressed to talk longer the components of the three-minute pitch could be expanded to thirty minutes by adding details of my methodology and stories. It wasn't long before I landed my first contract to help a travel technology and data services provider.

I was elated and excited about my new life as an independent consultant and determined to make this a success. I arrived on site at my first JPP client and met with the company executives to confirm the project's goal which was to reduce cost by outsourcing some of their operation and my role to help them through the selection process. Project detail definition to include the scope and timeline were also key components of these meetings. I was determined to strictly follow my methodology, and not waver on my values. I reviewed my methodology with them and received their sign-off and commitment that they would follow my approach.

That being settled, my next step was to kick off the discovery phase of the project. That meant documenting their issues, current processes, and collecting work volumes.

The client hadn't decided between India or the Philippines for the location to outsource their work, so we considered both countries. I learned through my past projects that the client may not have the correct information needed to make key decisions this early in the project, also that some of the executives may have preconceived ideas about the solution, which may be difficult to change. That prompted me to add a step at the beginning of my methodology, which was outsourcing education. I developed an extensive presentation on the state of outsourcing or Outsourcing 101, which included my list of best countries to send outsourcing work. Since I've added this step, it has been invaluable to be able to walk a prospective client or a new client through this presentation to set the proper expectations and help uncover any perceptions they may have. As you might imagine, the best places and companies to outsource work continue to evolve.

We spent some time developing their desired future state and vendor selection criteria. Next was developing the RFP or Request for Proposal document[19], and at the same time, I refreshed my list of outsourcing companies who would receive the RFP, which included companies from both India and the Philippines. With these two items developed and refreshed, I presented them to the company executives for approval. The only change was to the list of outsourcing companies to receive the RFP. The executives wanted to include a couple of their client companies on the list. This add on is what I eventually termed adding friends and family to the vendor list. The RPF was sent out and we waited for

---

[19] The RFP presents preliminary requirements for the commodity or service and may dictate to varying degrees the exact structure and format of the supplier's response.

the responses to come back in, as well as took questions from prospective outsourcers while they were filling out the proposals.

Once the proposals came back, we scored them to come up with our short list. While we were scoring the RFP response, a client executive wanted to add a company who hadn't receive the RFP because they didn't make the short list, but someone had told him they were good. As I said earlier the outsourcing landscape changes and I might have missed a company, so I agreed to add the new company. That meant contacting them, and if they were interested, sending them the RFP. We finalized our short list, including the new company, and started arranging for an onsite visit to include my client's project team and myself. This seemed straightforward, but once we notified the short list companies of our pending visit and the companies who didn't make the short list of their status the politics began in earnest. Outsourcing companies who weren't selected found every way possible to get to the CEO, CFO[20], CIO[21], or any executive they could find to plead their cases. The results were that only one additional company was added to the onsite visit list. That's when it became obvious the client's executives would bend to political pressure. I was still confident, because my methodology was flexible and could accommodate these changes, that once the short-listed outsourcing companies were properly evaluated, the selection should be obvious, but the executive's reaction told me the final decision may be more difficult to reach. I found out later that my client's parent company was advising my client's CEO on adding these companies. I understood that sometimes we must entertain a proposal from a legitimate vendor to keep our relations intact.

---

[20] Chief Financial Officer has authority over the company's finance operation and is the chief financial spokesperson for the organization.
[21] Chief Information Officer has authority over the companies use technology and data.

Putting politics aside, I produced a travel package with everything our team needed to properly evaluate the outsourcing companies, as well as the logistics and details about the cities our team would visit. We left on our long journey to Manila, Philippines and India which included Delhi and Bangalore. Our approach was to travel to a city in the morning, rest the balance of the day, and visit the outsourcing company the next day or evening, depending on the time zone we were in compared to when they performed the work for their US clients. The site visits usually lasted six hours. When we got back to the hotel after our visit, we would meet as a team, and each member would score the outsourcing company based on our selection criteria. Our objective was to have all the data to facilitate the final selection by the end of the trip.

The trip was exhausting, some of us had difficulty staying awake during meetings, with the time zone differences and busy schedules. The trip went well, and we had finished the scores for each candidate vendor with the top three scoring higher than their competition. Once back to the United States, we met once more to review our evaluations and then developed a report showcasing the top three companies. One of the first add-on companies scored in the top three and the political one scored at the bottom of the list. Next, we prepared and presented the results to the client's executives. We included the data for the top three, with the balance of the vendor's data in the appendix. It was clear as to which outsourcing company would best fulfill their needs. Our work was accepted as presented along with several clarifying questions.

Now the process went into the negotiations phase. During that phase, my role was to advise my client on the pricing, contract terms and conditions, and any other related items that might come up, such as vendor-dedicated resources versus shared resources. I believe the client has the fiduciary responsibility to negotiate their contracts (I chose not to take on that responsibility because I felt the liability was too great).

During the negotiations, politics reappeared. A multinational conglomerate company who offers outsourcing, but who scored at the bottom of our list, called the Chief Executive Officer of my client's parent company with a business suggestion. This low scoring vendor suggested that they might benefit from using my client's products and services and my client might benefit from using their outsourcing services. Their call meant, "pass that along to your subsidiary's executive team." Companies don't usually commit to guaranteed business up front, but paint the picture of the potential business opportunity, as in this case, and the parent company's suggestion carried a lot of weight with my client.

After a week's delay, my client's CEO announced to the project team his decision to go with the multinational conglomerate company. Afterword he asked me to join him in his office to explain the potential business they could receive with his decision. I understand business and my clients can make whatever decision they deem best, but why go through the selection process? "I understand making business decisions that best benefit your company." I said, I also reiterated the obvious issues that our evaluation brought out and my prediction that this decision wouldn't work well in the long run, but his decision was final. I thanked the CEO for engaging me for this project and sharing this information. I wished him and the company good luck and closed out my contract. The world of outsourcing is close-knit so information of who is being successful and who isn't gets freely shared. I found out later that, as predicted, their outsourcing decision didn't go well, and the outsourcing contract was short lived. The second negative that my client faced was they didn't get any measurable additional business from the multinational conglomerate company. They were left with calling the top vendor from our evaluations and engage their services. At least they had a vetted list of fallback outsourcing vendors.

The lessons learned in this engagement was that I needed to continue following my methodology, even though the client might make a different decision than the obvious one. Second, I needed to understand the starting point for my clients and to educate them as appropriate, and third, to understand that when politics get in the way, that doesn't mean I did a bad job.

It was September and I had finished this contract when I received a call from a global airline. The reason for the call was that they were evaluating consulting help to outsource some of their reservation's operations. After we talked on the phone for an initial interview, they invited me to come to their headquarters for a face-to-face meeting. I discovered they'd gotten my name from the CEO of my last client's parent company, a much-appreciated endorsement, I made my arrangements and flew to their headquarters the next week. That endorsement was uplifting and reinforced that I had done a good job at my last client.

Upon arrival in the airlines home base, I took a cab to their corporate office near the airport. I was greeted and led into an office for a two-hour meeting with the Senior Vice President and Director of Reservations. They first fired questions at me to see if I knew enough to continue our meeting and possibly make it to the next step in their selection process. After I had established my credentials, they explained the reason for the project. Their labor was costing them three times more per hour than it should, and they were experiencing a thirty percent absentee rate in their Reservation Centers. Reduced productivity and increasing cost are success killers. The solution they had in mind was to outsource some of their reservation's operation.

Next, I asked the Director to go to the flip chart and describe their vision of the solution. I've learned that knowing what and where the client thinks they want to go and/or where my competitor had convinced them to go gives me vital information on how to better help the client and sell my ideas by changing the game. As the Director drew out their vision, they said they were nervous about outsourcing, since previous management had sent some work to a U.S.-based outsourcing companies Canadian center, and it wasn't going well. Therefore, their approach was to start small by outsourcing their Frequent Traveler Program [22] member's calls. If that went well, they would expand to the Casual Traveler, which is a larger population. After they had finished explaining their approach and reasoning, I asked a question: "Why do you want to risk upsetting your most loyal and higher revenue customers in this experiment?" There was silence in the room for more than fifteen seconds while the Senior Vice President and Director looked at one another. The Senior Vice President broke the silence by say that changing their approach and starting with the Casual Traveler and not their Frequent Traveler, might be a more logical and less risky approach. The rest of the meeting was adding meat to the bones of the revised approach. The meeting concluded, and I flew back to Atlanta to await their decision. I learned they were considering several other companies for the assignment in addition to myself and the initial approach they laid out on the flip chart was an idea from another consulting company.

The next week I received a call from the global airlines saying I had won the business. They wanted me to fly back that following week to start work. I was elated with the new business so soon after my last engagement and I had beaten several competitors for the work. I immediately called Mark to see if he was available and would like to work this new project. He was available and said yes. This win along with my previous one gave me a fast start to my independent consulting practice.

I flew into their home base that next week, as directed, and first met with the Senior Vice President, who became my day-to-day contact on the project. During this meeting, I was told that I

---

[22] Frequent Traveler Program: airline benefits for flyers who travel from thousands to millions of miles.

had won the business before our initial meeting had ended. That is what we refer to in sales as a one-call close. They don't come along often, and I'm grateful when they do. During that meeting I also discussed Mark's role in this project. My client already had an expectation of me adding an additional consultant to the project.

My first two weeks on the global airline assignment was spent interviewing executives to understand their vision of the solution and to build support for the project. Before each interview, the Senior Vice President said, "This person is smart, and we need to listen to what they have to say." After the two weeks of interviewing, the interviews changed to people who didn't have a vision of the future but were being interviewed for political reasons. I concluded that we had enough executive input to proceed with the project and asked the Senior Vice President how many more people we needed to interview. I was anxious to get moving on the project, something that's in my DNA. Being told that I had an estimated couple more weeks of interviews, I couldn't resist asking a question: "So if all of these executives are so smart, why is this company in bankruptcy?" I calculated that the question would either get the project moving or get me thrown out of the account. The Senior Vice President <u>was</u> a very smart person, and my question got the project moving.

The thing that I learned from this was to always consider your advice as if it were your business and all the money was either going into or out of your pocket. Don't answer questions with what you think someone wants to hear. Answer questions with your best advice. Take the time upfront to do the consensus building but get the project moving. Also, it's okay to be frank with senior executives—they're people, too, and by asking hard questions, you can help them deliver a successful project. You are being paid to get results, so get them.

This global airline was a client for over three and a half years and twelve different projects, but the initial and biggest, which encompassed four of the twelve projects over a two-year period, was to outsource some of their Reservations and Customer Care Centers. The strategy was to still maintain some centers in the U.S., while closing several US and international centers by outsourcing those activities.

I approached these four projects confident of success and my abilities to drive that success. I knew my first task was to get everyone on the same page regarding scope, objectives, timing, priorities, and outsourcing knowledge—in other words, all the project organization, charter, and planning activities. Finishing this phase is important and satisfying to me because it provides focus and an alignment of purpose for the project team and executive team.

Next, we added the assigned company resources, which gave us the plan and resources in place, we were ready to start executing the project. The first phase included vendor selection process, a favorite part of these types of projects. I get the chance to visit prospective vendor sites and evaluate their operations. I use the fresh information to update my knowledge on vendors, their capabilities, and my vendor and country evaluations. Constantly updating my knowledge of vendors enhances my ability to provide best-in-class consulting to my clients. Part of the vendor selection is the location selection, also a part of my knowledge base. We worked through the large list of possibilities which included the issuing of a Request for Information (RFI) and narrowed the list down to those we wanted to visit. At this point, any team member or executive could add a vendor name without issues because we were collecting information. Over the course of the Reservations, Customer Care, and back-office projects, we visited vendors in, Nova Scotia, Hong Kong, Beijing, Guangzhou, Shanghai, Manila, Bangalore, Delhi, Mumbai, Pune, Dublin, Athens, Budapest, Bucharest, and Poznan. Maybe we should've gotten a t-shirt made with a list of cities our "band played" during this engagement.

During this time, we also visited several airline company locations, such as in Buenos Aires, Dublin, Hong Kong, Beijing, Mexico City, Montevideo, Sao Paulo, and Tokyo to evaluate their outsourcing needs. Again, these types of trips took their toll on body and mind because of the long workdays, flights and time zone changes. Exhaustion among our project team led to tension and sometimes tempers flaring. I admit I was guilty of this on a couple of occasions, which was unprofessional and inexcusable.

Many years before, when I worked for MSA/D&B Software, I had been diagnosed with psoriasis [23] which was followed over the years by physicians, prescribing various treatments and medications. The travel toll on my body and my psoriasis was significant. Hours before one trip to Latin America, I had an infusion of the latest drug for psoriasis. The drug's full impact was present by the time we landed in Buenos Aires resulting in severe joint pain. I had taken other psoriasis drugs which produced a reaction and was given prednisone to counter act my reaction, on this trip I didn't have prednisone. My stay in Argentina and subsequent travel to Uruguay was painful. I was glad that Mark was on this trip and helped me especially with my luggage. After that ordeal my instincts were telling me that I needed to find an alternative way to handle my psoriasis, I started a journey to find that alternative.

The vendor weeding out process was successful, and the finalists advanced to the short list phase. We then issued an RFP for these vendors and planned site visits. Once we received the RFP's back and vetted them, we set off on another world tour of vendor locations. I used the same approach of vendor evaluations

---

[23] Psoriasis is an autoimmune skin condition that causes itchiness and discomfort.

that I had previously. That meant we would finish the tour with our evaluations completed and the finalist, who would proceed to the negotiation phase. I say finalist, because the airline liked to negotiate with the top two on the list, something that is call a bake off. They feel this approach gives them more leverage. As I've said previously, my role in this phase is to advise my client on the pricing, terms and conditions discussed, because I believe the client has the fiduciary responsibility to negotiate their contracts. With the contracts negotiated and awarded, the number one vendor on our evaluation won the business. Then we began the implementation phase.

The airline had put together an excellent project team who had come up to speed nicely on outsourcing. My role during the implementation was advisor, coach, evaluator, and a pain in the vendors back side when they didn't execute properly or missed a deadline. The vendor selected had a robust new-client onboarding processes, which facilitated the successful implementations. Their processes included setting up the physical space and infrastructure needed, and the hiring and training of their employees. The training program was best of class which included such courses as U.S. enculturation, airline vernacular, and accent neutralization. Getting to know little things like the phrase "puddle jumper" is something that flyers in the U.S. understand, but it wasn't part of their vocabulary. Accent neutralization was fascinating to watch. It's the systematic learning of a new speech accent so the non-native speaker can communicate clearly. This is much like learning French or Japanese, where we adopt the accents used for those languages, except in this case various regional difference are removed and a neutral American language accent is taught. This neutralization is something that I learned without being taught when I went to U.S. Military dependent schools because we had students from many places with many accents which for me melted together to become something more neutral. When I started college people would ask me where I was from because they couldn't tell by my accent. I've continued to work on it during my business travels while speaking with clients for whom English is a second or third language.

The airline would eventually have outsourcing vendors in Europe, India, and China. As these vendors started servicing customers, the internal issue of expectations and misinformation came to the front. When a customer complaint came in at the executive level, the executives who weren't in favor of outsourcing would point the finger at our projects as the cause. In every single case, after it was investigated, the poor customer service came from the existing Reservations and Customer Care Centers in the U.S. and not the outsourced ones. Now I'm not saying that everything was perfect with the outsourcing vendors—they made mistakes as well. But those mistakes and complaints were most often corrected and handled at the local level. Overall, the implementations were successful, and my client saved tens of millions of dollars while greatly improving their customer service. These four projects were long and hard but satisfying because the projects stayed on track with my methodology, and they were successful.

During my first year with the global airline client the tipping point of a strained marriage came about, Sam and I divorced. I've thought about it many times since our divorce in 2004 still coming to the same conclusion, I was the primary one who caused the problem.

I was fifty-seven years old and rejected the idea that I was having a mid-life crisis. However, my growing age, inevitable mortality, having not accomplished things in life such as being a recognized photographer, learning to paint, and writing a book. At that time, life expectancy in the U.S. was mid to high seventies, which gave me around twenty years to accomplish these goals. Maybe this was a mid-life crisis.

I wanted to devote time to these pursuits as well as live in a more urban location where I was close to museums, the theater, music venues, and the arts scene. Locating from the suburbs to in-town Atlanta wasn't something Sam wanted. She was concerned about a lack of safety living in an urban environment might bring, especially because I was constantly traveling, and she would be alone. She liked going to artistic events but not nearly as much as I did and the travel into Atlanta was an hour or more each way.

My frequent travels took a toll on our marriage. Beginning in 1973, the series of jobs I had required travel and my international travels, which meant at the time of our divorce I had been on the road for over twenty years. The impact of traveling that much and for long trips evolved our relationship to where we were leading separate lives, and our differences had become more pronounced. It had to have been hard on Sam with me rarely at home and an unstable life.

After Sam and I divorce, we sold our house, and I moved into Atlanta in a thirty-two-story condominium building where I was close to the museums and theaters. I also used the in-town location to reignite my photography. I did enjoy these activities, but my constant traveling continued.

Sam purchased a single-family house near our former house and Jennifer bought a townhouse near her mom.

Life at the airlines continued with another memorable project, "lost luggage." The assignment was to review their lost luggage processes and report findings and recommendations. One interesting part of this assignment was that we had to go down in the tunnels under the hub airport. It turned out to be more than just tunnels - It's a whole city with streets, traffic lights, and carts going everywhere. It was amazing.

The process review started by watching the agents at the check in counter who logged the luggage into their system, attached a bar code tag on the bag and placed it on the belt which sent it to the underground maze. Once beneath the airport, luggage goes through a large circular scanner that reads the bar code tag and sends the luggage on to the gate so it can be loaded on to the correct plane.

We next looked at what happens when the scanner can't read the bar code, and It's sent instead to the luggage-rerouting office. A couple of reasons why the scanner doesn't read the bar code is that It's missing, torn off, or two pieces of luggage are butting up against each other and the bar code isn't visible. In the rerouting office the luggage worker tries to find the owners identification information by way of a personal ID tag attached to the outside of the luggage. If the owner identification isn't found, the luggage is opened to look further for the owner's identification. If the owner's identification *is* found, the worker goes into the reservations system to find out where the luggage is to be sent. The worker then creates a new tag, and off goes the luggage.

What happens if no owner identification is found? The worker searches the contents for a sample of identifiable items to put into the system in case the traveler files a lost luggage report, and various contents can be identified. Some of the identifiable items might be pink cowboy boots, bright yellow jacket, or just simple items like grey paints, blue blazer, three pairs of high heeled black shoes. Since the bag can't be forwarded, it goes to the lost luggage warehouse. The airlines hold the luggage for ninety days and if it can't be reunited with its owner, it's sold to a third party. The third party can then resell the luggage contents. All of this seems organized, but in our report, we recommended several improvements.

One of the first improvements involved the agents at the check-in counter. When the luggage bar coded tag is printed, there are several small bar code tags printed as well. The suggestion was for the airline agent to take the smaller bar code stickers, which weren't being used at that time, and place them on at least two other surfaces of the bags to better ensure the scanner picked up the bar code and properly routed the luggage to the departing plane. This recommendation was implemented.

The second issue is a more of a job performance one. This issue was detected when looking at the luggage in the rerouting office and noticing three identical large yellow bags. Obviously, they belonged to the same family because they were all the same size, color and marked with the same color ribbons tied to the handles. When questioning the worker in the luggage-rerouting office, he said that sometimes the baggage handlers don't want to handle heavy bags, so they cut the bar code tags off. Thus, the bags come to the luggage-rerouting office where they're hopefully retagged and reunited with their owner. The act of removing tags seemed futile, because the same luggage handler could end up having to load them onto the plane anyway. This issue was brought to the attention of management as well, who promised to address it with the baggage handlers. Confirmation of that discussion wasn't provided by management, and it was disappointing to have to make this recommendation because it shouldn't have been happening. It was also a symptom of why the airline was in bankruptcy.

The third step in the lost luggage review process was to visit the claims processing office and luggage storage warehouse. The claims office processes financial reimbursements for lost luggage and sells off luggage that has been in the warehouse for ninety days. We noticed the financial reimbursements process was a little backlogged, but travelers did get compensation for their lost luggage. We made suggestions regarding stream-lining the processes and cleaning up the backlog. After the ninety days, the luggage that is sold usually goes to a single source who buys the luggage by the pound. That source for my client was an operation in Alabama who resold the contents in a large retail facility. So, if you lost your luggage, you might find it at one the resellers. The interesting thing about global airlines lost luggage is that it cost them tens of million dollars per year but, since that's just a small piece of their operation expenses, it could go mostly unnoticed—once again, a symptom of their financial predicament. But I can attest that it doesn't go unnoticed by anyone whose luggage has been lost.

The overarching recommendation was to focus on an exponential improvement in customer service and reduced lost luggage frequency. A step in that direction was the recommendation to increase the number of customer service agents and shorten the turnaround time handling claims, in person, on the phone, and via email. That recommendation was met, but with pushback from management. They wanted cost reductions not cost increases. Some companies lose sight the balance needed between customer produced revenues and internal procedure control. Both are needed to deliver bottom line results. In this case, improving customer service and performance of the operation will lead to a better customer experience, more repeat business, more sales, and profits.

My lessons learned on this project, were: First, it only takes a few seconds to do the job right the first time. Putting several bar codes on the bags reduces lost luggage. Handling the bags for the first time and not cutting off tags reduces lost luggage. Second, I've always been a believer in managing by walking around. My reasoning is that you can stay in touch with things and understand the magnitude of issues better and focus on the areas needing improvement. Not to mention, if you ask the workers their suggestions for improvements, you will get a lot of good information. If management stays in their offices or does just "touch downs"—very brief—visits to the operations, they will miss many opportunities for improvements. These opportunities can result in savings and increased sales, putting tens of millions of dollars on the bottom line.

In September 2005, I took a vacation to Paris, France. Mark and I were over half of the way through the difficult airline projects, which ended a little over a year later, and my divorced had been less than a year before, as usual for me I had continued to work long hours on the airline projects and didn't take the time to recover, think, and relaunch my future. It was time to visit my beloved Paris, a city that brings back fond memories and where I'm comfortable, to reflect, charge my batteries, be alone, and pursue one of my favorite things to do, photography.

I arrived at Charles de Gaulle airport at six a.m., secured my luggage, made my way through Customs and Immigration, and found a taxi to my hotel. I had traveled to Paris many times since the days I'd lived there, but this trip was about me and getting reconnected with life.

While traveling to my hotel the taxi driver asked me a couple of questions and I responded in my limited French. I noticed the driver kept look at me in his rearview mirror. He finally asked if I was French, I replayed that I wasn't, but American. That conversation was a nice welcome back to Paris. At least I had a decent accent when using my limited French.

The taxi dropped me at Hotel Prince de Galles, and checked in, complements of Marriott, since I had hundreds of thousands of points—there *were* a few perks for the millions of miles I had traveled. I spent the rest of the day walking around the city shaking off the jet lag, had a great dinner at an off the path Italian restaurant, and went to bed, early.

The next day I ate breakfast, grabbed my camera, and headed out for the full day of taking photos. Since I knew Paris well, I didn't have to think about where to go for my photo shoot. I went to the Eiffel Tower, Sacre-Coeur Basilica, Left Bank, and many more photogenic places. The day was hazy and smoggy which would require more post processing of my photos than normal. After shooting several hundred photos I decided to call it a day and go back to my hotel arriving around four p.m. I went to my room, loaded the photos into my laptop, and was shocked. The photos were horrible. It wasn't just the haze and smog, but the composition was poor. I didn't understand what had gone wrong. The photos were of the intended subjects but were drained of passion and life.

I decided to go to the bar, have some wine, and try to figure out why my photos were crap. After a glass of wine, I asked the waiter for a pen and some paper to capture my thoughts. While working on my second glass of wine the thought hit me, I had gone through the motions of taking photos that day, rushing from location to location. I was rushing to get "a job done", like I do at work. I hadn't been in the moment and didn't *feel* the photos. In short, I wasn't fully engaged in taking the photos and they were lifeless. I didn't follow the advice of professional photographers like Ansel Adams who talked about getting beneath the surfaces, Ralph Gibson who suggests seeking a relationship to the subject, and Elliott Erwitt who says photography is an art of observation.

I asked myself why I had attacked this *assignment* that way. I then realized the language of my question alone held the key. This was an assignment that I attacked to get it done—not a loving pursuit of creating beauty with photography. I realized that this was the way I had handled most everything in my life—attack the assignment to get it completed. In the business world that works, but it didn't for my personal and creative life.

I came to Paris for a refresh and a reset. To do that it required a review of the past and the lessons learned. I spent the next couple of hours reflecting, writing, and drinking wine, but not too much wine because I was writing more than drinking.

The summery of my writings that day in the bar:

<u>Reflections</u>: My life has been defined by Duty. I had let life pass by and all that it has to offer for the sake of getting it done, duty. Duty meant doing what was expected of me. Duty was working hard and providing what other people wanted but, not *what* I wanted. Duty was working sixty-seventy hours per week and not taking care of my family or myself. I've done other people's bidding, so what have I learned? I've learned that a value system has many aspects and components. All these aspects and components must be equally shared and no one value should dominate your life. I started to question the accepted norms for success and to craft my own.

<u>Apologies</u>: I offer my apologies to my family, my friends, and my associates for not doing and saying the things I felt.

<u>Getting it right</u>: Now a new beginning and a chance to get it right. A chance to be true to myself and my loved ones. To balance my life and give something back. I'm in Paris, the city that gave me a new life while in high school, allowing me to grow far beyond where I would have had I stayed in the U.S.

<u>What is next</u>: I've a lot of things in my favor, a loving and beautiful daughter, great parents, good friends, and an optimistic attitude towards life. I'll develop a new set of principles that are balanced and reflect my true self.

The next day I went out in Paris to be in the "zone" and to feel the inspiring photos. At the end of that day, I reviewed my shoot, the images were full of life, emotion, and beauty. At the end of the week, I flew back to Atlanta with a renewed focus on life.

After three and a half years Mark and I finished the airline projects and moved on to other opportunities. I generally don't like to work that long with a client without a break between projects. The break prevents a client from considering me an employee who can be given additional assignments that take my focus off the project at hand. A break allows everyone to close out the last project and concentrate on starting the new one. I'm not saying that being considered as one of the family is bad, and it's appreciated. I just like a clear beginning and ending.

CHAPTER 13

SUCCESS & LOSS

Managing an independent consulting business requires me to stay in touch with resources like Mark, Ron, Norma, Ricci, and Keith so if I need help on a project, I will know who was available. On one occasion I asked Mark if he knew what Ricci was doing since she went off on her own path after MSA/D&B. At that time, I knew Ron, Norma and Keith were all working and not available. Mark said he would get in touch with her and set up a lunch meeting. A few weeks later the three of us had lunch during which Ricci said she hadn't consulted for six years and was an artist now but would consider coming back to consulting if she liked the project. As we left the restaurant Ricci took us to her car and pulled out some of her paintings to show, which made me curious. Before we all shook hands and departed, I ask Ricci if I we could talk again about how she became an artist, she agreed.

I had a growing interest in the arts and had talked with other artists in the past few years since my divorce, but each conversation was discouraging. On one occasion, I was at a dinner and had the opportunity to talk to a mid-thirties artist who explained she spent half of the year in Atlanta and half the year in the western US painting. When I said I would like to learn to paint, "Well you had better be willing to spend seven to ten years of study before you can start to paint," the artist replied. That suggestion seemed too ominous to consider. I asked a follow-up question as to why one couldn't start painting and learn as they went. "Oh no, you have to learn to draw, and you must know colors and pigments, textures, bushes, paint types, mediums, and the strokes of the master's before you can hope to produce a painting," was the answer. I asked how this artist learned these things and the reply was by following a formal art education. That encounter was repeated several other times which is why I wanted to know the path that Ricci had followed since it didn't seem to be the same.

Ricci's art journey wasn't the same, she was mostly self-taught. She did take various short-term classes with artists to learn their techniques and she also had an art coach for a while. The difference with Ricci's approach was that she was creating works as she was learning. I'm not saying that a formal art education wouldn't allow the creation of works as the student is learning but Ricci's approach was more flexible. I started spending more time with Ricci, as my consulting business allowed, and created my first 12 x12 painting in March of 2010. My assessment of it was horrible, but it was fun to create a painting. My education expanded when Ricci introduced me to various galleries and artists. Each visit with an artist or a gallery was inspiring and helped me to see what could be created.

These artists were more accepting of anyone who was interested in art even though their background was a long road of creating art and growing along the way, some had formal education, and some even had a parent who was an artist. One of the introductions was her coach with whom I started taking classes. These were one-on-one classes as I worked on a painting. The first technique he taught was to "let the canvas paint itself," he would say. The exact technique was to wet a canvas with water by hand, then brush on a single color with varying degrees of thickness and leaving some white canvas showing. Once dry, I outlined any figures I saw, then turned the canvas forty-five degrees outlining what I saw from that view, continuing until I had come full circle. From those outlines I would start painting with other colors to darken the outlines and fill in the figures, adding shadows and other accents. This approach helped me to relax my business drive to control everything, as Ricci would remind me.

Learning to paint and the techniques used gave me a better perspective on my photography by teaching me to see more of the detail and the whole picture including the often-overlooked sides of the photo when shooting. I was on my way to fulfilling my painting goal, which I thank Ricci for her guidance and encouragement. That was one of her missions, to help people fulfill their artistic dreams.

My next client came when I was introduced to an auto-parts retail and distribution company. They primarily do business in the United States but have some operations outside the country.

I met with an Executive Vice President to discuss their business needs and to determine how I could help. We agreed that I would perform a savings opportunity analysis at their distribution centers, accounting centers, procurement group, retail operation, and two technology groups, totaling six business units. The objective was to identify the savings opportunity at a high level only. This initial study would help to determine if a detailed analysis was worth doing, and if so, determine the priorities. In conjunction with my client, we selected a sample set of operations to collect data. We included operations that were regarded as good performers, bad performers, and middle of the road performers. Even with limiting the sample size, there was still a lot of work to be done. I contacted Mark to assist in the collection of data, onsite visits, and analysis. I didn't know it at the time, but this project launched a relationship with this client that lasted over sixteen-years and twenty-nine projects.

The project launched and we started visiting facilities. During a site visit for this initial project with one of the company's Vice Presidents, was talking to an office employee, he noticed the person wasn't following one of the recent procedure changes sent out from headquarters. When he inquired as to why, the employee said, "Yes, headquarters sends out a lot of changes but there's not enough time to read all the bulletins and do anything about them.

The workload is too heavy, so we do what our General Manager tells us to do." He thanked the employee, but I could tell this answer was like a stomach punch to the Vice President. "I can't believe what I just heard," he said to me as we walked off.

In the rental car on the way back to the airport, he reiterated that he couldn't believe the headquarters bulletins with important policies and procedure changes were being ignored. His expectation was that if the bulletin was sent out, then things would change immediately. He also believed that these bulletins were helping both the processes and the work being done at the local level. I told him I would investigate the situation as I visited other locations.

I investigated and found that the bulletins were, in fact, burdensome. Usually, the changes added more steps within a process, and more manual tracking and checking, which meant more work. In some cases, the change was a result of a single problem that occurred in a single location, but the company felt it was important to write a policy and process to apply to everyone. The lesson in this was to understand the impact of your actions. Sometimes the "help" resulted in doing more harm than the original problem. It's sometimes better to correct the single problem at its source, rather than generalize the solution.

Because I had asked Mark to join me on this project, we were able to divide the detail workload but collaborate on the conclusions and recommendations. The project started in 2007 and lasted four months. In our conclusions and recommendations document we identified numerous opportunities for improvement. For example, productivity was low and averaged less than 40%, costs were higher due to absenteeism and turnover, there were company cultural and political roadblocks, and customer satisfaction was inconsistent. The recommendations also included the centralization of various duplicate processes, the outsourcing of some technical services, and the consolidation of duplicate offices. The client greatly appreciated our analysis and recommendations. As for me, I was excited about having uncovered opportunities, as it's rewarding to help a company improve the service and profitability.

But I also want additional work from the analysis, and I submitted a proposal in September 2007. Doing these types of analyses can result in one of three things: I get immediate additional business–which is what I want; the client decides they can do the follow-on work themselves without help (not an outcome I want) or I get more business over a period, so I must have patience. In this case, it was the third result, when I started the distribution detailed analysis in 2010, but other recommended work didn't start until 2011.

In October of 2007 I decided to go with my dad and mom to the Veterans Hospital in Atlanta to get an update on my dad's ongoing health issues. The doctors continued over the past year to say he had walking pneumonia. That didn't make sense, and I wanted to get answers. We met with the doctor, he put dad's x-rays on light box on the wall and told us that dad had cancer with only three months to live. I jumped in with questions about why dad and mom had been told it was pneumonia since it was obvious; by looking at the x-rays, he had cancer that spread through his body. "I'm new here and I've just looked at this case, but the x-rays seem to show the cancer has been growing for a while," the doctor said. I knew that dad couldn't get any better by me continuing to ask why, so I stopped. The doctor then reviewed dad's options. Of course, chemotherapy was the next step but, even then dad's life expectancy was in terms of months. Mom and I were devastated but dad was still the tough soldier. "I'll get through this," he said. It wasn't until years later at a time when VA Hospitals overall were under fire for poor treatment of veterans and this VA Hospital was in the news for reports of malpractice and mismanagement that I realized dad's problems had been going on for a long time without proper treatment.

Mom started the arduous task, but with love, of driving dad for his frequent chemotherapy treatments from their home in Woodstock, GA to the Veterans Hospital in Decatur, GA a seventy-mile round trip. In late November dad was getting worse, and hospice was brought in to treat him at their house. Mom called me on December third to say I should come to stay the night when hospice told mom that he may not make it through the night. On December fourth he passed away. Prior to dad's illness I couldn't imagine a parent wouldn't be on this earth with me. I knew they both would die someday, but not just now. It did happen and my hero had left the earth.

During my business travels, I worked with several outsourcing companies in India. From time to time, I would get calls from their CEO's asking questions about the industry and seeking advice. On one such occasion the owner of a business process outsourcing company called to seek advice on how he could grow his business. He had three other companies that had grown to be ten times the value of this one company. We talked for some time about his opinion of why this company had a growth problem and his vision of where this company should be from a market share, revenue, and profit. He also wanted to answer a key question, should he build the company or sell it. At the conclusion of our discussion, I suggested I spend two weeks with his management team in India to develop answer his question and develop a plan implement the solution. We agreed and I coordinated with his management team to schedule my trip. I had gotten to know this team during my previous visits, and I knew how to work with them to get this assignment completed. Because of my previous work with them, I already knew several areas where they could improve the operation. We set the schedule, and I flew into Delhi where a hotel was arranged near their corporate offices.

I expected that when I arrived our first meeting would generate many questions and some pushback from the top executives as to why I was asked to come in instead of the owner asking them for a plan. As expected, my first meeting onsite was with the subsidiaries CEO, someone I had known for years. We discussed and ironed out any issues with me coming in versus them doing the work on their own. We agreed he would be the executive on the project, and I would manage the day-to-day. He and I reviewed his preliminary selection of employees to be on the team and came up with our final list.

I was getting settled into an office when the CEO scheduled a kick-off meeting for an hour later. The project team was assembled, and I went through the project assignment, goals, timeline, and settled on their specific assignments for the research, analysis, and plan development. I also got the CEO and teams agreement that they, not I, would present the plan to the owner. I wanted them to get credit for the work and the results.

The research part was the most difficult. We had to collect information that would answer the owner's question about selling or investing to build the company without sending shock waves through the India business community. The business community, in this case the outsourcing business community, is a tight one where rumors circulate at the speed of light. Our project was to be kept confidential. This type of research we were doing is like completing a several thousand-piece puzzle. It requires going to many sources, including NASSCOM a well-respected, thirty-year-old, non-profit IT and Business Processing Association. With each source you get pieces of data that must be verified and assembled into the mosaic needed for our recommendations.

The team performance was excellent. Within the two weeks a large amount of information and data was collected and analyzed. The team developed projections on growth by market, trends on future markets, their current business and profitability, and much more. The job was so thorough that when other outsourcing companies and the trade reporters got wind of the work, they were calling to request our information. Of course, no information was given out for competitive reasons. After two weeks of long hours, we were ready to present the findings and recommendations. In our last-minute push before our one p.m. meeting, we had lunch sent in from the cafe in the building. I had a cheese flatbread with bottled water. That meal would angrily come back to me later that evening and on my trip home the next day. When the anger came, I started taking Cipro[24] which got me home.

We were ready. The subsidiary CEO, part of our project team, kicked off the meeting with introductions and purpose statement. He then called everyone's attention to the thick book we had developed during the project, containing this meeting presentation and all the detailed backups. We chose to present three scenarios: 1) Aggressively invest and grow the company, 2) Keep doing what they had been doing with little investment and modest growth, and 3) Sell the company and get a return on the initial investment.

He then went through the three scenarios concluding with the team's recommendation of the aggressive investment and growth option. The presentation went well with good business questions being asked for which the team was well prepared to answer. At the conclusion of the presentation the owner thanked everyone, but with an obviously angry expression and tone of voice, asked one final question of his team; "Why had you not already done this work and why did I have to call John in to get it done?" There was dead silence and finally the subsidiary CEO said, "We didn't know you wanted us to do it." The owner's response was, "It's your job to do this work and I shouldn't have to tell you to do it." The owner's question and his team's previous question of me at the start of the project were the same but from

---

[24] Ciprofloxacin s a fluoroquinolone antibiotic used to treat a number of bacterial infections.

different perspectives. The answer was simple, they used a top-down controlling management style and not a collaborative one. This type of style limits the forward thinking and planning of the lower levels within the company. With both parties asking the same question, I took the opportunity to recommend additional internal alignment training and individual skills development work be a part of their investment and growth plan. The final decision was to implement the aggressive plan. The company went on to grow this business to over thirty delivery centers in thirteen countries and added another business to their portfolio, a regional airline. This project resulted in a company moving forward and hopefully the management team improved their working synergy.

There are many dynamics in every organizational structure that are a roadblock to collaboration and cohesiveness. The lesson here is that companies need to actively work on their internal success engine, alignment, atmosphere, and management styles. The goal of the top executives should be to give clear direction and communicate without over managing.

I once worked on a global project for a well-known market research company where corporate office was giving clear direction, but their field operations weren't complying. Their payroll cost was too high and needed to bring them down. After many tries to get the problem under control without results, they felt it was time to call in consulting help.

That is when I got the call and flew into the headquarters for a planning meeting. We agreed on an approach that would first determine their actual employee headcount in their key office locations as well as some suspicious offices, but not all fifty-four, office locations. I was to visit the key locations and especially the locations showing more data anomalies. The smaller locations only had two or three employees, and it was easier to perform the headcount review without going onsite. One of the visit locations was the Singapore office. I set the dates, made travel arrangements, and set off. I showed up at the office at 9 a.m. to meet the General Manager. I had to wait because the manager didn't come in the office until 10 a.m. I spent the time reviewing my reports of that location and talking to the office employees. When the manager came in, he was upset that I had arrived early. I reminded him that his confirmation email specified 9 a.m. His approach to me was one of jockeying for position, a well-recognized tactic to gain power. I find that insecure managers sometimes like to use intimidation tactics, but they don't work with someone who've had real-world experience. It was also not a good move on his part since the authorization for my work and visit came from his corporate office with his regional Vice President's blessing.

After I didn't back down in our tete a tete, I explained that this project was one we were carrying out globally and visiting medium to large offices. I presented a list of employees for the Singapore office which had been produced two days before, and I needed to meet each one to verify the headcount. His reaction was to challenge my list saying that things change all the time, and my list was probably out of date. I told him that wasn't a problem, and he could give me his list of current employees. He pushed back, saying, "This will take time to produce." I countered his challenge by saying, "I don't understand since headcount and high payroll cost is a concern of headquarters, I would think that you would have a handle on headcount and have a list of current employees." Even with my challenge, it took him four hours to produce a list. By then it was mid-afternoon before I started to meet employees and check them off the list.

As a representative of headquarters, I took the opportunity to ask each employee how things were going, and if they had any suggestions for improvement. To many, it was a shock to have someone ask their opinion. I knew it wasn't the custom in Asia, and obviously it wasn't something being done in this office.

Because of the delayed start I came back the next day and the day after to continue the count.

On my final day, I got down to a handful of unverified employees. I approached the manager to ask where these people were and how I could get verification. The manager continued his subterfuge by making excuses. After going back and forth with him for what seemed like an hour, I said that if these people couldn't be verified, they would have to be immediately removed from the payroll and I would advise payroll not to make any future payments to them. I could tell I had found his phantom headcount because arguments were emotional and without logic. I immediately contacted the project executive at company headquarters to advise him of my findings and to counter any communications coming from the local manager.

Once the dust settled these unverified employees were removed from the payroll. Removing them meant that money wasn't being paid out to nonexistent employees and headcount costs were lowered. As I had seen before, people who try and pull off something shady will be found out because when pressed they give themselves away by their actions. I heard later that the manager was removed.

CHAPTER 14

ATTEMPTING CONSISTENCY

In 2010 I began the Distribution Center (DC) detail work which was one of the largest projects I would have with this auto-parts company. The project was to review the back-office processing, productivity, and cost. The objective was to assess the feasibility of centralizing these processing from over fifty DC's, which were spread thought out the US. The reasons for this project were three-fold, first they wanted to focus the DC's on selling and delivering products to their customers, second, they wanted to deliver a more consistent back-office performance and service, and third they believed the decentralized costs were too high. If the three objectives were met, they believed this would improve both the customer's experience and their bottom-line profits.

I'm always excited to start a new project. I can see where we're going and what it will look like at the project's conclusion. In other words, visualize its success. As an independent consultant, I don't like taking a project if I'm not excited and can't see the benefits for the client, I usually turn it down. I didn't have that luxury when I worked for large software and consulting companies.

Because objecting to a project with questionable outcomes didn't result in rethinking the commitment to do the project. It was usually met with comments like, "Gut it out" or "Make it work." This meant that I had to aggressively reset the client's and my employer's preconceived expectations of the outcome. In projects with questionable outcomes, I had to dig hard for any semblance of success. The reset expectations were usually met, but they weren't the clients or my employer's original expected results.

Also, there are times when a client's expectations of the outcome are way out of line with reality. Resetting those expectations, as I've said before, is difficult but needed for the client to get the best results. I also prefer projects where I can stay until the finish, not just perform the analysis phase. When I get to stay for the implementation, I can be a part of driving success, not just to give advice. My style is to push the project team, which means I make people uncomfortable, nervous, and occasionally angry. My bottom line is if you can't deliver a success, don't take the job.

After the organization phase of this project, we moved on to the detailed information collection phase since we already had the high-level analysis from our previous project. That included collecting information on the client's past project successes and failures. I've discovered that more projects are unsuccessful or get cancelled than I would have thought. Each project has its own specific reasons for failure. Some of the reasons are a lack of qualified people on the project team, insufficient allocation of funding, company restructuring or new management that changes priorities in the company, a constant internal assault against the project because people didn't want it in the first place, and there are turf wars. Many times, it's a combination of several of these success roadblocks. Sometimes an executive has an idea—not a good idea, but no one will challenge doing a project around this bad idea. Why start a project if you aren't going to deliver a success? When these questionable projects move forward, they have a higher probability of failure or at least, don't produce the results anticipated.

To be successful, even with good ideas that are doable, takes fighting in the trenches every day to pull them off. This DC's back-office project had all the potential for success and failure unless there was continual executive support and an aggressively managed, that was the approach I took. There were times I had to overstep my consulting role to get to the goal.

We pulled together a five-person team, trained them on the project approach, and went to the first DC to collect detailed data. We planned on staying two weeks at the first center to test our data collection sources and methods. Before going in we developed a list of back-office processes the DC was responsible for performing. Onsite, we collected a list of what processes and other tasks each office employee performed. We then collected the transaction volumes and how much time it took to do each process. We ran into many roadblocks in collecting transaction volumes because these numbers weren't numbers that had been collected before, meaning no reports were available. Trying to get computer generated reports of what little system data existed was difficult because the people who would write the reports had other assignment priorities. We improvised and found, through colleagues, a way to get access to internal systems and pulled some of the information ourselves. The balance of the data came from our team going to file cabinets and stored boxes to collect transaction counts.

Another issue, although predictable, was when we sat with employees to understand what they did and how long it took to do the work, we were met with the human element, that's when some people try to influence the analysis. Some wanted to impress us with how fast they completed their work, some had developed shortcuts to their work, but others some wanted to show how hard the job was and why it took them a long time to complete. Our objective is to find out what is needed to get the process done well. Our team sorted through these roadblocks because of their experience doing these processes, by doing multiple observations, and cross team observations, which meant, that at times, more than one person on our team observing the same employee. At the end of our two weeks, we had modified our data collection model, better understood the roadblocks, and succeeded in not significantly ruffling feathers while at the DC.

I also walked away with some observations that would prove consistent throughout the balance of the DC's our teams visited. I say teams, because we expanded our data collection to four teams of three people each to tackle the balance of the work. I took the assignment of analyzing the overlapping of tasks between these DC's, headquarters, and other central processing centers. Also, processes differed within a DC causing tracking of performance to be more subjective and not measured by statistics. The team's calculation of productivity averaged between thirty-five to fifty percent, even after adding a ten percent contingency factor. The productivity numbers weren't as high as they should've been. Back-office operations differed considerably from location to location, and the staffing levels in each location couldn't be correlated with the levels needed to perform the processes. We concluded, the opportunity for improvement was tremendous.

These opportunities weren't surprising, given the background of how the company had evolved. Each of these distribution centers had started as autonomous operations. Each location chose to use their people the way they saw best, resulting in inconsistencies from location to location and minimal standards across the company. Personally, I believe some autonomy is good, but when the tasks performed feed central systems, standards are needed. Remaining totally autonomous wasn't advisable.

We also encountered a lack of buy-in from the distribution center management when faced with losing more autonomy. They had already experienced what they consider a loss of autonomy when previous projects had moved work out of the field and centralized at corporate or another single processing center. DC management wanted to keep work that they believed was their responsibility and that their customers demanded. Their argument was their customers wanted only them to handle all their needs locally was a myth. I debunked this myth by visiting the several of the distribution center's customers and asking them what was important in handling their needs. Some of the customers were cooperative while others were defensive. A few customers almost told us to get out of their operations when we announced we represented the company. Their attitude changed when we told them we were outside consultants. Then it was "great what do you want to know?' This group of customers were brutally honest. The customers confirmed that selling and delivering the goods purchased should be done locally, but that back-office work needn't be. Their comments confirmed, my previous findings, that customers want their issue, request, or question to be handled correctly and timely regardless of where It's performed. They also said that contacting their local distribution center didn't always get the job done. One customer went so far to say. "If I call the DC and don't get a certain person on the phone, I'll will hang up and call back later, because this certain person is the only one there who actually gets things done." Client's just want the job to get done. The myth was debunked again.

Our data collection uncovered other anomalies, such as employees being misclassified in the Human Resources system by job and departments. Normally, just changing their data in the system would correct the problem. But the administrative task of changing an employee's assignment, in the system, wasn't a top priority at the distribution center level. There are several reasons for this view: It's not seen as vital to their mission to their customers, the assignment may be considered a temporary one, the operation is lax on administrative duties, or the local management reasoned it didn't matter since the overall payroll cost was the same.

In one distribution center we found several employees were assigned to the office in the budget but were working in the warehouse. The local Operations Manager became upset and pushed back hard when our team questioned the use of these employees. This Operations Manager wasn't known to be shy and retiring, and the issue escalated into a battle. At the end of the battle, our team prevailed, and the employees were moved to the warehouse budget. The opposite was also found employees working in the office but were assigned, in the system, to the warehouse or some other non-office job. Again, their reasoning was why did it matter? But it *did* matter because performance against departmental budgets were being measured and since headcount was being pulled out of the office and centralized, it was important to know exactly the amount of headcount and work should be moved or should stay in the DC.

Even though the back-office centralization project was viewed by some as another one to strip the locations of authority, many Distribution Center General Managers view it as favorably because it would reduce their cost and deliver better and more consistent customer service.

With our data collection phase completed, we moved to the analysis phase. This analysis would recommend what processes should be centralized and what should remain in the DC's. Additionally, new organization structures and staffing levels were developed for the centralized service center and the distribution centers. Our teams came from many different parts of the company and there were differences of opinion that lead to animated discussions during our analysis work. There were a couple of team members that objected to pulling out any headcount from the distribution centers and their data collection showed it. After one of our animated discussions, I discarded their data and assigned other team members the task of reassessing the processes. After the reassessment, and no coercion on my part, I accepted the revised data because it was consistent with tons of data already collected. Since this assignment was voluntary, we did have a turnover of a few team members However, the teams produced a solid business case document with the details for implementing at the centralized service center and each of the distribution centers. Our document was presented to the corporate and field executives, again with much discussion, but was received favorably. Even though it wasn't until 2013 that the project to implement our recommendations would start. I did get the business to work that project.

In 2011 I received a call from another area of the same company who asking me to come in and start implementing the first of the projects identified in the 2007 analyses. This project was to develop a business case and plan for four accounting and technical support operations detailing how those services could better be provided and at a lower cost. Given the volume of work I called Ricci and asked her to participate in the project. She was available and agreed to join me. Mark was working on another project and wasn't available, but I believed that Ricci and I could handle the work.

These were four operations where duplications appeared to exist. The genesis of these multiple operations came from, as before, the company's decentralized past when field management wanted support as close to their physical location as possible, believing they would, have more influence over these operations and get action quicker. But that wasn't cost effective, nor did it lead to better service.

Upon completing the business case, the data showed that the duplication of operations wasn't needed and in fact inconsistencies within and among each operation was becoming more pronounced, not to mention the cost savings potential. My recommendation was to consolidate into a single operation each, one for accounting and one for technical support. After executive review and field management discussions my recommendations were implemented. There was one exception: the Personal Computer configuration function was better served by outsourcing. This group handled the setup of new equipment by installing a standardized image per company specifications, this was a service the PC manufactures offered prior to the new equipment being shipped. Management decided to go with that option and negotiated a contract with their preferred brand of equipment.

As I've said and will continue to say, finding opportunities and helping to bring those improvements to reality is something I love to do.

The summer after completing this project Ricci who wasn't only a painter, but a writer went to Tybee Island, GA to attend a women's writing retreat for a week conducted by her writing coach Rosemary Daniell, founder of Zona Rosa. Ricci and Rosemary invited me to the retreat's close-out party at the end of the week. Attending that party, in addition to being fun, was the first time I got to meet several published authors including Rosemary Daniell, who would become my writing coach. At the party some of the attendees of the retreat were asked to read a sample of their works which were outstanding, and they also performed a musical skit. The party was mainly in the living room, dining room and kitchen, all of which was packed with books and artwork. On the dining room table lay a collection of the latest published books from the group, impressive and inspiring. I pitched in by helping with the refreshments in the kitchen and while I was getting acclimated to the layout, I noticed something odd in the microwave. I opened the microwave, I found it was full of books; I couldn't stop laughing. I've been fortunate to be invited to this fun and inspiring event many times since. Like painting, meeting and talking to authors made me more excited about writing. For years I had wanted to write a book, I even came up with a few book ideas, gave the ideas a title, and mocked up book cover for each. As Ricci had done, in the painting community, I thank her for introducing me to the writing community and her support of me pursuing writing.

I continued to spend time researching alternative solutions to my psoriasis issue. My improvements began several years earlier when Sam and Jennifer encouraged me to start exercising, even with my busy travel schedule. At the time my weight was two hundred twenty-five pounds and even with my six-foot frame, the weight was too much. I began a regiment of working out at the gym and running, which enabled me to drop down to one hundred ninety pounds.

I've entered many races including fifteen Atlanta's Peachtree Road Races[25] held every Fourth of July, but have never entered a marathon, maybe that is still a possibility. Another area that Sam and Jennifer encouraged me to pursue was diet. Not just dieting to lose weight but to eat the good things and cut out the bad. Jennifer and I belonged to the same gym and at one point she suggested that I take advantage of a food sensitivity test they offered. The results were mind blowing, I was eating things that were inflammatory to my body and not helping my psoriasis. I ended up developing a large spreadsheet, my friends laugh at me for my love of spreadsheets, containing my good foods. Foods that didn't impact my psoriasis or food sensitivities, while making sure I excluded foods with high toxicity. The one factor that was almost impossible to remedy was stress. I felt that something was missing in my stress elimination research.

I turned to Ricci, who was also an Herbalist, to get her advice. She said she would start researching but I should also go to some herbal conferences to gain more knowledge. In 2012 I attended my first conference with Ricci and have attended several conferences since. I learned about the plants and their contribution to my health. I also learned about environmental factors in my personal life that are toxic. That lead to me taking various herbal remedies which were helpful, but my learning journey continues.

---

[25] 10k Road Race held on July 4th with tens of thousands of participants.

The next project with the auto parts retail and distribution company came in 2013 and was for phase two of the distribution center back-office consolidation project identified in 2010. Ricci and I worked the project along with a good team of employees from the company. Our assignment was to first validate the business case previously developed, second to develop a detailed implementation plan, and third to coordinate the roll out of the implementation. The desired scenario for the consolidation of the back-office work was to create two central service centers resulting in a cost savings of ten million dollars. The direct customer interfacing, customer service, sales and delivery, tasks were left at the field locations. Several other, nonbusiness critical tasks were eliminated. The Service Centers were to focus on their assigned processes and build a center of excellence for those processes. Our team worked with the company's Human Resources department, and they were able to move a lot of the affected field DC employees to other open positions within the company.

As the rollout took place over nine months, there were exception requests and challenges that arose. Even though there was upfront agreement, sometimes managers change their minds when it's being implemented in their operation. A comment I often heard was, "I agree we need to do this, but my location is different, we should be an exception." Each challenge was reviewed, and if adjustments were warranted, they were approved. We all know that these types of changes are hard, and they become harder when they're close to home, but we all must change or get left behind.

The selection of where the two new service centers were to be located was a subproject. The team developed, along with executive input, the site selection criteria. We looked at current internal facilities, external facilities already built out, and external facilities that would require building out. After the analysis was completed, our recommendation was to use two existing internal facilities, one on the East Coast and one on the West Coast. The reason for the two centers was that field management wanted a center close to their time zone for what they perceived was better customer service. Even though, the best practice shows these centers can be located anywhere because they staff for all needed time zones. The service center model of an East and West coast facility successfully operated for six years until improved systems and additional automation were introduced. At that point all processes were consolidated into the East Coast service center, delivering additional savings. The project ended with all objectives being met, more focus on servicing the customer, more employee productivity, and dollars saved.

CHAPTER 15

ADVENTURE & SADNESS

The service center project being completed I started seeking other opportunities to help companies improve their performance. I still lived in my Atlanta condominium, Sam had moved to Tennessee and worked a part-time job at the Tennessee Welcome Center and Jennifer had started a new career in corporate real estate management.

During my marketing efforts to find a new project, I received a call from a search firm who was recruiting for a head of operations in a small, privately owned consulting company. Because of my past experiences working for a company, I had misgivings, but the idea sounded interesting. I wasn't going to abandon my consulting company, but it might prove to be financially lucrative, and the recruiter said the company wanted to go public the next year. I agreed to go on the interview with the owner and several of his executives. I again approached this opportunity with a wait and see attitude, but when offered the job I accepted. Things were going well for several months, then I started to see the owner lash out at various managers and consultants. After asking around, I learned this was the norm. When people made a mistake or did something that wasn't exactly the way expected, harsh criticism came their way. This style may get an immediate action but is hardly long lasting.

I also concluded that in some of the approaches and methods used for estimating and committing a cost savings number to the client was difficult to deliver. Some projects did deliver large dollar savings, but not all. I tried to assert leadership but that was short circuited by the owner. It became obvious to me that this was another bad situation, that I had told myself I wouldn't get into again. As you can guess, the owner and I started to disagree on many things including the way I was handling my job. The result was that I was let go. As we've heard, in life when you learn a lesson, don't repeat the same mistake again. Clearly, in this case I did repeat the same mistake, by chasing the money rather than following my commitment to my own company.

Shortly after that misguided side trip, I was called by my previous client, the auto-parts company. They wanted my help on another large project, which had previously been identified and recommended, to improve the productivity of their corporate payables and receivables service center. The center had been in existence since the mid 2000's and had reported to several different functions and business units over its history. The objection to these processing centers as I mentioned earlier doesn't always go away over time, therefore continued criticism was the case with this center. It didn't matter whether the criticism was valid or not the two sides were firmly locked into their position. The field locations said the processing center was making mistakes, and the processing center side was claiming the field locations were making the mistakes. I was apprehensive about helping this center because I had visited them in the past and made several recommendations for improvement, none of which had been implemented. In addition, I knew that they were super sensitive because of the field criticism and were firmly entrenched in their belief they were doing things correctly.

My showing up on-site to perform this improvement project wasn't met with enthusiasm. I had gotten the assignment from the executive ranks with the approval from the processing center director. But the mid-managers and supervisors weren't a part of that decision and didn't like it. The managers took a firm position that they needed more people, and not process improvement since they managed their departments efficiently.

My position was to do a data collection and analysis, and then all interested parties could evaluate the results and make appropriate decisions and I would make a recommendation as well.

During the data collection phase started immediate roadblocks were thrown up by the processing center mid-managers and supervisors. There was criticism about the data collection approach, and I was told the needed data wasn't available, requested information was partially provided or in some cases not at all, and scheduling time to observe employees kept changing. The one good thing was when I called a meeting of the mid-managers and supervisors attended. Apparently attending meetings was something they all were committed to do even though most brought their laptops and seemed to be working on other things the whole time.

The processing center was an open design so one could see at least half of the operation at any one time. I could stand in the open space and observe the pulse of the facility. I observed many people constantly walked around and talking to coworkers at their cubicles. As I walked around, I heard more social conversations than business ones, and the pulse was more social than productive. The social atmosphere, along with time away from their desks attending company events, led me to conclude productivity was lower than advertised.

When the data collection and analysis started to come in, we held meetings by department manager to review and discuss the results. In some cases, the managers would agree with the individual employee results and in some cases disagree. When they logically disagreed, the employee and process observation was repeated, and data reassessed. In less than 5% of the time, the results were altered—many times because the data initially provided by the department was incorrect. Before the final report was completed, another meeting of the respective department managers was held to review the results. The final reports showed an average of less than 50% productivity. At this level of productivity, tasks weren't getting done or they had too many people, and additional staff wasn't needed. This company, and so do many companies, believes in the concept of working managers. That means the managers have their own specific tasks to perform in addition to managing. I've always maintained that approach is flawed. I believe that managing is a full-time job. Managers should be coaching, training, and finding ways to continually improve their operation's performance. In this case, the managers were snowed under with tasks, which left little time to manage.

The analysis did find a few employees who were at or above the 75% level of productivity, or what I call burn-out level. In one review meeting, I made the statement about burn-out and how it might be impacting a specific employee, at that point the Human Resources manager said that a particular employee had resigned just resigned. Truly knowing the productivity level of each employee can raise the low performers, highlight process issues, and lower the burn-out cases, which reduces turnover. I've found that most employees want to do a good job and feel better when they do, it's managements responsibility to provide the training and coaching while eliminating the barriers to success.

In this project, I wasn't engaged to stay for the implementation of the recommendations — the processing center management took on that task. I do know that some staff was reduced, some processes were improved, and some savings were gained. The lesson here is that to be a high performing company you must work on reviewing, measuring, and constantly improving. Managers working heads down on tasks starts to narrow their vision and it's harder for them to come up with improvements. Providing opportunities for them to observe and study other top performing companies provides ideas and inspiration. This sounds simple, but it isn't. Just the day-to-day work can consume a manager's time and improvements get pushed to the side.

While this project was winding down and projected to be completed in April of 2016, Ricci was taking a trip to China in May of that year with a group of Herbalists and wanted me to join her. The reason for the trip was to study Traditional Chinese Medicine at Shanghai University for two weeks which included classes and hospital rounds at Longhua Hospital. I jumped at the opportunity to accompany her so I could spend the time catching up with a friend who live there, take photographs and furthering my knowledge of China, this would be my third trip.

The itinerary called for us to fly from Atlanta to Beijing arriving on May 14, 2016. We landed the mid-afternoon the next day, connected with another group member and took a taxi to the hotel. We were tired from our nineteen-hour trip, and so upon arrival we checked in, ate in the hotel restaurant, and went to bed. We knew it would be a busy two weeks and the next day we were sightseeing all day.

The next morning, we left the hotel early on our nonstop tourist adventure fully stocked with sanitary wipes, toilet tissue, and water because the sanitary conditions away from hotels are challenging. I usually don't like to participate in group tours in favor of striking out on my own. In this case it was better to go along with the itinerary, get to know our follow travelers, and the organizers were able to get us into sights that I couldn't have done on my own. Our first stop was Tiananmen Square, the location of the 1989 student-led protests which started in April and ended in June. The Chinese government declared martial law and forcibly shutdown the protest which included firing on the students and using tanks to retake Tiananmen Square. It's unclear as to the number of dead and wounded but, most accounts put the numbers into the hundreds or thousands. Our guide also told us that all records of the student protests had been erased. What most of us remember is the picture of a lone protester standing in front of and blocking the advancement of Chinese Army tanks.

As our group walked around the crowded square, filled with Chinese tourist wanting to see the Mausoleum of Mao Zedong, his final resting place. The security force in the square were young men with short hair, wearing white shirts, black paints, and the same sunglasses. This differs from my previous trips, where the security force wore standard military uniforms. On previous trips there were squad and platoon size army troops marching in the square. Some were relief for the guards stationed in the square and some were there for overall security of the area and Mao's mausoleum.

Our tour continued as we walked across the street to the Forbidden City, which we were told, served as the home of Chinese emperors and the ceremonial and political center of the Chinese government for over 500 years. The city is magnificent containing hundreds of buildings within its just under two hundred acres and its length of over two miles. Yellow is dominant because it was the symbol of the royal family. It can be seen throughout, roofs, ceilings, and decorations. The city is a great place to take photos, and I took hundreds. Even though this was my third time touring the city I know I still missed some special shots. While at the Forbidden City some of our group needed to use the restrooms and were shocked by having to use the squat toilets, a hole used as the toilet where you place one foot on each side and squat and deposit the wipes and tissues in the waste basket next to the toilet. Everyone now understood why they had to carry the wipes, tissues, and water.

We only stayed at the Forbidden City for a couple of hours because we had to eat lunch and leave for the Great Wall. My lunch was disappointing, so I didn't eat much and had one of my protein bars later in the day. Meals while on guided tours in China are a challenge. The tour guides want to provide a western version of their county's dishes instead of offering the best of their cuisine. Sampling the real food of the country means having to go off the tourist route and on your own. As we walked to our bus, after having lunch, there were vendors selling hats, t-shirts, umbrellas, water, and all sorts of tourist items. The day had grown hotter and several of our group bought these items. I admit I got a Chinese sports cap, even though I had a baseball cap in the hotel room, which didn't help now with the sun beating down.

The bus picked us up just off Tiananmen Square for our ride to the JuYongGuan section of the wall located in the JuYong mountain pass, forty miles northwest of Beijing. The bus traveled through the busy streets of Beijing before getting on the Badaling Expressway, which is a direct route to the Badaling Great Wall section. The Badaling section of the wall is popular and contains the Museum of China, National Forest Parks, and other popular attractions. Our destination of JuYongGuan, eighty percent of the way to Badaling, is significant as one of three fortifications built to repel invasions through the JuYong pass. This section was rebuilt during the Ming Dynasty to protect the northern borders from a Mongolian invasion.

Leaving Beijing the expressway is three lanes on each side, traveling past industrial, commercial, and residential sections of the city. Once we reached Nankou the lanes narrowed to two each way. The vibrant green mountains with light brown rocks jutting out started to narrow in on our expressway. At that point we were three miles from the JuYongGuan Great Wall. Once we reached our exit the wall was in front of us, it was so close it seemed like it was built as part of an expressway rest stop. After exiting the expressway our route took us under the wall on the way to the bus parking area.

Arriving at the staging area each of us decided what part of the wall we wanted to see and hike. Our group then set off individually or in small groups along the walls two-and-a-half-mile long perimeter and fourteen watchtowers. Some chose to go to Watchtower 13, the highest point, with an elevation gain of just over one thousand feet, the climb is rated as "hard" by hikers.

Those of us who didn't climb that high found other viewpoints to see the magnificent mountains, valleys, and the way the wall snakes along the hills on its thirteen-thousand-mile journey.

The view was gorgeous with the green and light brown landscape and the clear river running through the valley. The day was sunny, temperature mild, blue sky and a few snow-white clouds strolling by. I took advantage of the great photography opportunity by taking a lot of shots. The wall is labeled an achievement of man costing ninety-five billion dollars, in today's money, and the lives of an estimated four hundred thousand workers, many of whom are buried in the wall. The question does get asked, "Was it worth it?" Times were different then and we're individually different today, each of us are left to drawing our own conclusion.

After a few hours everyone met back at the Great Wall Café staging area where we enjoyed ice cream, sodas, coffee, and snacks. Being tired after an exhausting day didn't mean we could rest because when we got back to Beijing, a Peking Duck dinner was planned for us. Bed that night felt good!

The next morning before leaving for Shanghai we visited the Temple of Heaven, a place I hadn't previously visited. Again, our guide was great and explained the temple was formed in the first half of the fifteenth century and it symbolized the relationship between earth and heaven. The temple is said to be "the most representative example of Chinese ritual architecture and the Hall of Prayer is one of the world's largest medieval wooden structures." It also is considered to reflect the mystical cosmological laws believed to be central to the workings of the universe. The park surrounding is lush with trees, shrubs, and flowers where people stroll, socialize, sing, dance, and practice *tai chi*[26]. As we were leaving the Temple through the park, we saw an interesting group of at least ten couples dancing a choreographed routine. The women were wearing olive green camouflage tops, red skirts or shorts, a green cap with a red star. The men wore black shirt with a Chinese flag on the pocket, black pants, and a straw Trilby hat[27] with a green camouflage band.

It took about thirty minutes to travel from the Temple of Heaven, fifteen miles away, to the Summer Palace. Our guides presentation about the Summer Place was excellent. The Summer Palace was originally constructed as an imperial garden by Emperor Qianlong to celebrate his mother's birthday. This location isn't to be confused with the Old Summer Palace, just two miles away, which had been mostly destroyed by fire. The Summer Palace is the place where emperors and empresses spent their leisure time and a retreat during the hot summer months. The Summer Palace covers a little over one square mile, three quarters of which is water. The guide said it was an example of Chinese garden design that balances architecture, horticulture, water, land, and pathways. Standing in the garden with the beauty surrounding, removed from the busy life outside, I felt a tranquil feeling come over me. It reminded me of my times in the gardens at the Rodin Museum in Paris.

Our time at the Temple and Summer Palace was short because we wanted to have lunch before going to the train station. We stopped at a retro restaurant, a flash back to the days of Mao. The food turned out to be good and was welcomed before our five-hour train ride to Shanghai.

The bus dropped us and luggage off at the Beijing South Railway Station. The station is a large oval-shaped station

---

[26] Tai chi is an internal Chinese martial art practiced for self-defense and health. Known for its slow, intentional movements.

[27] A trilby is a narrow-brimmed type of hat once viewed as the rich man's hat.

designed by a British architecture firm. The inside was modern and crowded, it can dispatch thirty thousand passengers per hour. We had our tickets but there was still a queue to go through security. Once onboard the train was much like an airplane, we were in second class or coach to us, with a two and three seat configuration, slightly reclining seats, tray table, and an overhead space to put bags.

There were screens updating us on our speed, location, and time. I glanced at the speed and location from time to time and saw the speed would go to one hundred eighty-eight miles per hour but go down as we travel through stations or populated areas. Several times while look out the window I saw an empty city or *ghost city*, as it's known. I remember seeing tall modern gray concrete shells of buildings, some not completed. The streets were void of people, vehicles, or any signs of life, except for one where I saw a car and a person walking. Several miles down the line we passed another bullet train track being constructed adding to the already fifteen thousand miles estimated to grow to twenty-four thousand miles by the early 2020's.

We arrived in Shanghai late in the evening, went to the hotel and missed dinner. Luckily there was a connivence store around the corner where we found snacks and bits of food. It was quite a sight to see ten hungry Americans descending upon this small shop.

The next morning Tuesday, May 17, it was time for our group of students to start attending their classes and do their hospital rounds. I walked with the group to the Longhua Hospital which was only a few blocks from the Lee Gardens Hotel because I wanted to know where to go in case I was to meet up with the group for dinner and any other reason.

After leaving the group I went back to the hotel, picked up my camera and started a ten-day photo shoot of Shanghai. A photography technique that I love is to walk the streets and take photos as opportunities present themselves. Not only do I get candid shots, but I get to know the area I'm walking. I started near the hotel and each day I increased my photo area. I took photos of shops, alleys, people, street vendors, buildings, laundry hanging out to dry on lines attached poles extending out from every floor in a building, and interesting signs. Every construction site I passed had government posters on the temporary walls surrounding the site.

One poster I saw showed a blue grey image of a Chinese woman kneeling, looking to the sky and holding a bird constructed out of paper in her two upwardly facing palms attempting to release the bird. The poster read, *"Release China. A dream is a hope sown in spring. The dream is the painting screen of the revival of the people. Realize my Chinese dream. The whole world listens to spring!"* The phrase comes from Xi Jinping, the General Secretary of the Chinese Communist Party. Chinese Dream is the "great rejuvenation of the Chinese nation." It has become widespread in official announcements encouraging young people to "dare to dream, work assiduously to fulfill the dreams and contribute to the revitalization of the nation."

Another poster showed what appears to be a three-person family collecting and storing eggs and grain. The caption read, *"Frugality and morality (are) national savings. Consciously save a grain of rice, a drop of water, a drop of oil. Start with one kilowatt hour, one piece of paper and one penny."*

A third poster promoted the World City Day of October 31, 2015, with these phrases, *"Better City, Better Life, Urban design to create livable spaces, Designed to Live Together"* and showing artists rendition of new skyscrapers.

I was one person in the group that had time on their hands during the day and frequently asked to pick up items various people needed, such as a camera storage card, a shirt, handheld voice recorder, or jacket. Therefore, during my photographic walkabouts, I visited several High-rise malls to purchase these items. The malls specialize in the products they sell, like electronics, clothing, eyeglasses to name a few. Several group members were interested in getting new glasses which meant four of us visited the eyeglasses mall for an eye exam and new glasses, ready within a couple of days, at reasonable prices.

The next day I was out taking photos on the streets of Shanghai. My destination that day was the area called the Bund, I had researched the area and picked up various pamphlets in the hotel lobby. The following is a summary of the information I collected.

The Bund stretches about one mile along the west banks of the Huangpu River, which is a seventy-mile tributary of the Yangtze River just before it spills into the East China Sea. This area came to be because of the 1842 Treaty of Nanking where the Chinese were forced to open trading and settlements to the western powers, these areas are also referred to as foreign concession areas. The buildings that developed over time are eclectic. Romanesque, Gothic, Renaissance, Baroque, Neo-Classical, and Art Deco are some of the revival architectural styles present along the Bund. Between these buildings, Zhongshan Road just in front of them and the river is a buffer zone with trees, shrubs, flowers, and a mile-long promenade. This promenade is loved by residence, tourists, and a popular place where couples go to have their wedding photos taken. Standing on the promenade, which is elevated, the green space and older buildings on one side and the new modern high-rise buildings across the river in Pudong District on the other is an awesome site. The most recognizable building on the Pudong side is the Oriental Pearl Tower. It looks like a spaceship sitting on a launch pad. The tower is fifteen hundred thirty-six feet high and consists of eleven big and small spheres. It has fifteen observatory levels; the highest is one thousand one hundred forty-eight feet high and is known as the Space Module. At night the whole tower is lit with brilliant colors. There are three other well-known skyscrapers on that side of the river, Jin Mao Tower, Shanghai World Financial Center, and Shanghai Tower. The tallest of these is the Shanghai Tower completed in 2015 and stands one hundred twenty-eight stories.

Thursday, May 19, I had an early dinner with a business associate who lives in Shanghai for the purpose of catching up and to also get a better understand of the current situation in China. After catching up my next question was, "Tell me about these Ghost Cities." It seems that the Chinese government wants to reduce the overcrowding of tier one cities and disperse the population. By building these shell cities they want people to buy them and move, he explained. The problem is that Chinese people love real estate. They buy these unfinished apartments, where the buyer must complete the interior, in their hometown for the pride but, they may not make it their permanent home, he continued. This was like my experience in France during the 1960s. Our new flat was bare, and we had to fit it out with no compensation for the effort when we left.

The topic turned to my curiosity of the Chinese government's strategy. His answer was straight forward and what I had expected, they want to preserve their long-term security, so their plans are always developed for the long term regardless of the ups and downs of the world economy. That approach is different from the United States who operates on a more short-term strategy. He believes the eventual outcome is that China will be _the_ world dominant player. The government operates like a bank, investing in and owning many things around the world and that ownership gives them the control, he added. That investment is something I would experience later on this trip when visiting a herbal granules manufacturing company.

I also learned from my research that China was buying up as much of the world's natural resources, concentrating on rare earth minerals, as they could and are moving into developing countries to offer their construction capabilities. He confirmed that my research was accurate.

I said goodbye to my friend and asked if he was still committed to China, his answer was yes. He and his family were still committed and had no plans to move back to the U.S.

After breakfast on Tuesday May 24, I met Emma, our Chinese guide, in the lobby entrance of Longhua Hospital at eight a.m. The evening before when Ricci came back from the hospital, she shared with me that this hospital is the number one hospital for psoriasis in China. Emma had offered to help me check in and after that I could see a doctor specializing in psoriasis. The first thing after meeting Emma that morning was getting her help to fill out a medical history and current medical issue in the Chinese Medical Records Booklet. The check-in hall was enormous, it had been built in 1960 and the style was marble, glass, stainless steel and had been well kept. We survived the mass of people, two hundred or more, and saw there were eleven queueing lines. We selected a line and worked our way to the check-in window. I handed the attendant my Chinese Medical Records Booklet and waited for the person behind the glass to say something. That's when Emma addresses the attendant and explained my purpose for being there. The attended told Emma how much I needed to pay, eighteen RMBs or two dollars and seventy-five cents, while she was printing and stamping my receipt. I also received a magnetic stripped hospital card and instructions to the Dermatology department.

Emma had to leave me to get back to her other duties and I went off to find the doctor. Upon arrival in the Dermatology department, I handed my booklet, receipt, and magnetic card to a check-in attendant, was then told to sit down and I would be called. I only waited a few minutes when I was called into the doctor's room. The room was small, plain white walls, one table against the side wall, and three chairs. I was greeted by the doctor and asked to sit down between the doctor and a scribe who entering our conversation and doctor's instruction into a laptop. The doctor didn't speak English, and I didn't speak Chinese, which didn't bother me because of my many previous encounters with people in the same language situation. As I expected, we were able to communicate with facial expressions, gestures, a few English words, and a couple of Chinese phrases I learned prior to this consultation. I was asked about stomach issues, sleep, stress, and diet, the normal things to ask. When I told the doctor about my diet which included a lot of chicken, she stopped me and said, "No chicken". I looked quizzically at her, and she repeated, "No chicken". She wrote down her comment and explanation in Chinese so I could get it translated later. The translation said that she and other doctors, in the hospital, considered chicken an inflammatory food, not good for psoriasis.

Once the consultation was over, I received a prescription printout and directed back to the check-in hall to pay for the medication. Doing so and obtaining a receipt, costing one hundred seventy-two RMBs or twenty-six dollars, I proceeded to the pharmacy, I turned in my prescription, showed my receipt and waited. It didn't take long, my name was called, I was handed a plastic bag with my prescribed tea granules. Medications are usually in the form of tea granules, teas are a common way to consume herbs in China, granules keep a long time, and refills can be easily shipped to the patient. The overall experience was pleasant, I spent a total of one hour and a half from entering the grand hall to walking out with my tea, at a cost of twenty-eight dollars and seventy-five cents.

In the morning of May 26, our students took part in the graduation ceremonies at Shanghai University of Traditional Chinese Medicine (TCM) and received their certificates for completing the TCM Clinical Training Course. After lunch we boarded a bus to Tianjiang Pharmaceutical Co., Ltd. for a tour of their facilities. This company was established in the early 1990's with financial assistance from the Chinese government and today is a world leading manufacturer of full-spectrum Chinese herbal extracts, concentrated Chinese herbal granules, with sales over one billion dollars. Our tour was fascinating, there were few employees, so I asked the question about how many employees worked at the plant. Our guide said they had started with several hundred employees but as they expanded their business, they automated a today only had a few employees. Their next physical expansion, under construction, would be highly automated and would only increase the employee numbers by a few. We met with the Chief Executive Officer for a briefing and dinner in their executive dining room. She said that their relationship with the Chinese government continue to be good and the government was helping them with their latest expansion. I asked and was told that the herb granules I was given at Longhua Hospital came from their plant.

My education of the complete process from source to manufacturing to hospital to patient was completed the next day when we toured the Yida Herb Garden, which contains over five hundred herbs growing the garden. After having lunch at the garden, we toured their museum which traced the practice of herbalism from its beginning. The museum contained a full display of multimedia, ancient herbs in glass containers and an array of ancient herbal medicine cabinets and processing tools.

This trip to China was even more rewarding than my previous trips because this time I had time and opportunity to spend getting to experience and understand this country. Throughout my trips to China, I laughingly noticed the Chinese people were taking more photos of us Americans than we were taking photos of them.

I was still living in my Atlanta condominium; Sam was still living in Tennessee and Jennifer had purchased a two-story house in 2017.

As I get older, I increasingly get the word that more people I knew have passed away. Such was the case in March of 2018 when Ricci passed away. She was visiting her sister in New York state and upon returning to Atlanta she was feeling ill. The next morning, she felt worse, so I took her to the emergency room at Kaiser Permanente. After several hours the emergency room the doctors decided she should be admitted to the hospital for further diagnosis, but her insurance company Kaiser Permanente had to make that decision and select the hospital. It wasn't until late that evening before she was sent to Northside Hospital in Cumming, Georgia. Her stay at this hospital was almost two weeks where she underwent numerous daily tests. The doctors finally concluded that she needed a more specialized evaluation and care. They recommend a move to a more specialized hospital, again the insurance company had to make the decision and late in the evening she was transported by ambulance to the University of Alabama Hospital in Birmingham, Alabama rather than an Atlanta hospital providing the same specialty. In Birmingham she underwent extensive and painful testing and was still not getting any better. Her condition kept deteriorating and at the end of the second week she passed away.

Ricci had a large impact on many lives. I think about our lively political talks, her introducing me to new foods, herbs, painting, Native American Culture, and writing. I think about her encouragement for me to actively pursue my photography. The loss was devastating! Ricci had an amazing spirit about her, she was truly a free spirit. Unfortunately, her body betrayed her spirit by failing. The 1964 song We'll Sing in the Sunshine sung my

Gale Garnett reminds me of Ricci's spirit. Her life with us was too short and after her passing we remember her by saying "we sang and laughed every day and then she went away."

CHAPTER 16

NEEDLE'S EYE

Three months later, I was asked to take on one of the most challenging assignments at the auto-parts company, which was five projects under one umbrella, a Productivity Enhancement initiative for the company's largest subsidiary. The five were two field operations projects, a central service center project, one for central accounting support, and a Human Resources Project. My role was project office leader to coordinated with the individual project leaders.

These projects were a result of a corporation wide initiative to reduce cost to get the profit ratio in line with revenues. It was estimated that these projects would save approximately three million dollars. The corporate executives were committed, and therefore putting pressures on those below them. The main person driving it was the Chief Financial Officer. She was the perfect person for the job—someone who consistently strived for improvement and innovation. It was exciting to work with an innovator who was focused on results. The individual project leads were also motivated but questioned why I had been brought in to oversee the initiative. They each thought that they could work well on their own and that the extra oversight wasn't needed.

Nevertheless, I was in the role and set about working to support them while reporting the progress to the executives. Over time some relationships developed, and resistance diminished slightly. I knew going into this assignment that it would be difficult because of the different business areas involved, the different agendas, and egos. People at these levels in companies usually have large egos and want, sometime insist, on directing the action. These challenges extended to the auxiliary groups such as the corporate process improvement and information technology groups supporting the initiative, even though they were in favor of me taking the role. During and after each meeting I received coaching on approach, priorities, tracking, and managing the initiative from various executives. I believe their motives were well meaning, even though I had managed many large projects for the company as well as several hundred projects with other companies. Occasionally I would get good advice, helpful feedback is always welcomed.

I also knew these projects would get push back and a lack of buy-in, mainly from the levels below the corporate executive ranks. These levels had already experienced what they felt was too much interference from the corporate executives and wanted to be left alone to run their operations.

However, that wasn't to be in this case. Straight out of the block, correct headcount data was again a key issue to solve. I've encountered the situation of correct employee headcount and assignments many times and have seen companies spend millions of dollars trying to get this under control. Companies approach employee assignment and headcount as differently as their cultures. Some companies go to the detail level and want each employee to have an approved job title, task list, and performance measurements, while the other end of the spectrum only looks at the total employee expense and manages that to the budget.

The detailed approach, the more prevalent, requires more administration, using enterprise software systems. However, it does provide more information to manage the employee allocation and support the company's goals and objectives. The high-level approach makes the total expenditure easier to track against budget. But it doesn't necessarily ensure employee allocation to support the company's goals and objectives, a more decentralized approach. This company uses a more detailed approach but there are compliance issues which lead to bad data.

The five projects, even though they all wanted to improve processes and cut costs, had their own unique complexities that had to be management separately. An implementation plan was developed along with what we thought was a clean headcount list and was signed off by executives and regional management as well as Human Resources. As the approved implementation rolled out at each location many of the actions were again challenged by local management.

The first of the field operations projects, scheduled for completion in two-years, was to automate many of the tasks being performed by employees at the distribution centers who tracked operational procedure and lost prevention compliance. What that meant was that some seventy people who were receiving forms, reports, receipts, and so on, from each of the stores to compare against a check list. In other words, did the stores do the work they were supposed to do? The company had this process because somewhere in the past, they had found some store managers weren't doing their job, so they put in this process of checking their work, rather than disciplining those who weren't complying or automating the checking process. The project goal was to eliminate the manual checking by automating the essential checking process which would result in better manager visibility, oversight tracking and a cost saving of millions of dollars. However, the project had technical programming resource issues that delayed its progress. Technical resource issues are a ongoing problem for many companies. In this case the technical programming resources are allocated based on a committee's determined priorities. Those priorities are influenced by company strategy, goals and objectives, and politics. When I left the project, the delay was at the one-year mark beyond plan.

The second field operations project was to revisit the previous implemented Distribution Center back-office tasks, and headcount reductions that had taken place several years earlier. It was common knowledge that headcount was slowly increasing, and a review was needed. The main question to be answered was whether the additional headcount was needed to support the business changes, or just to increase the size of their organization? Our challenge was again inaccurate data on employee assignments and headcount. As before, the official roster of employees, which had previously been labelled as official, hadn't been kept up to date, requiring several rounds of review, debate, and negotiation to get a clean list for the project. Human Resources wouldn't take on the ownership of the numbers but laid the responsibility of accurate headcount on each field manager, after all they were the source of the data. After getting the clean employee list, the discussion centered around what was the level, roles, and structure needed to support their current business needs. This took an additional amount of time, analysis, and negotiations to finalize the approved headcount and positions. The project was completed after a couple of months and resulted in a workforce cost savings a couple million dollars.

The third project was to close one of the two central shared service centers on the East and West coasts established during the previous project. The reason for the consolidation was that most of the work had already been absorbed by the East Coast Center, and their operating hours had expanded to cover the West coast. In addition, the West coast employee cost, turnover, and absenteeism was too high to deliver the original cost savings goal. One of the reasons for the high turnover was a shortage of labor in that area. Employees could easily leave our center and go to a higher paying job, in a location closer to their home. A plan was presented to corporate executives, field executives and management to gain their approval. The only small objection was from the Distribution Center management where the West Coast Service Center was located. During an onsite conversation with the center's management, they admitted to getting faster and more preferential service by having the center in their building, all they had to do was walk over to the center request various actions be taken and the center would quickly comply. This was, of course, not a reason to keep it open.

The difficulties of shutting down an operation are many. This operation was in California, so the numerous regulations and paperwork associated with this closure and must be handled properly. The plus, in this case, was that the center was inside an existing distribution center and several company retail locations were in the area. That meant that those employees being let go could apply for jobs in the warehouse or one of the stores.

The consolidation took a couple of months longer than planned because of hiring, training, and new employee productivity ramp up issues. The biggest part of the delay was again a shortage of qualified labor in the East Coast site area and a lack of full support by the companies recruiting and training functions. Despite that, the consolidation took place with three quarters of a million dollars in savings.

The fourth project was a process improvement and headcount reduction for the field and headquarters accounting functions. The headcount was small and potential savings were minimal, but the impact on the overall streamlining of accounting process were worth the endeavor. Resistance to this change came from the long-term manager. They felt and defiantly stated that they had continually improved their processes and didn't see any reason for the change. A key factor in moving forward was the upcoming retirement of the manager of the field accounting function. The accounting executives wanted the replacement manager to be a part of any change, so unlike the other projects, this one became stalled out for the time being. Still, a little improvement was made with minor savings impact.

The fifth project was in the field Human Resources group. The objective was to reduce cost in this function and management's thinking was to move the field payroll processes into the Employee Shared Service Center, which was already in place. We kicked off the cost reduction project and the first order of business was data collection and analysis. I used my 2012 detailed field process improvement study and an additional analysis of the various tasks the field human resources managers and staff performed as the base for meeting the objective. The combined studies showed, as expected, that there were significant differences by location. Each manager's tasks varied because they were being influenced by their local General Manager. In some cases, they were viewed as additional administrative staff and not as contributing to the success of that operation. In other cases, they were viewed as a contributor to the operations success. This wide variation needed to be changed to be more consistent.

It was clear that Human Resources function needed a transformation into one that contributed to the success of the operation and not just an administrative one. In addition, the company had a severe turnover problem, and needed to revamp the recruiting, hiring, on-boarding, training, and retention program. During my discussions with human resources management, I recommended that three key areas be targeted for improvement; centralizing payroll, solving the turnover problem, and contributing to the company's success should be handled as one project. However, the pressure was on immediate cost savings and management thought that dividing the three suggestions into three separate projects with different timelines was a better choice. That meant payroll centralization came first, and the others could wait. To me, separating the three projects was disappointing because this was the opportunity to make transformational changes to the field Human Resources function to deliver the potential overall cost saving and value that refocusing would bring to the company.

The central consolidation of payroll was kicked off by an excellent Human Resources Director whom I've worked with for years. The project was being implemented at a pace compatible with the Employee Service Center's ability to absorb the work and still be successful.

While I was working on the five projects, I consented to oversee a short proof of concept assignment to demonstrate the capabilities of a financial tool the company wanted to implement enterprise wide. The assignment: take a small process and show how this tool could replace an older one and would also have the capability to do a better job. I met with the internal business analyst assigned to do the work to determine the work effort. The analyst said the work was uncomplicated and estimated it would take four weeks for it to be completed. Given his explanation, the estimates seemed reasonable, so we scheduled our first internal client meeting.

The analyst had been working in the job for about a year. His background was as a back office financial manager, but his knowledge of internal consulting was limited. But he was the only one available with the knowledge of the financial software and was strongly recommended for this business problem. I quizzed him at length, and he seemed to understand the project approach, based on what we knew at the time. If he followed the analysis process, the project would have a better chance for success. But I was still uncomfortable with his inexperience in helping clients solve problems. He had had a few projects with mediocre results and was anxious to come up with the perfect solution to make this project a success.

The analyst took the lead in our first client meeting by reviewing and confirming the project scope, objectives, and the source of the data needed. We finished with everyone in agreement, and the work began.

During our next project update meeting in which the business analyst was to present how far he had gotten with the project. I had been checking in with him along the way and was told we were on track. During this meeting, the business analyst started asking questions about its scope, objectives, and data source. The participants and I were confused. Hadn't the scope, objectives and data source been made clear in our first meeting? In addition, had the business analyst been giving me false reports over the past two weeks? Apparently, he hadn't grasped the assignment. The analyst and I had a meeting afterword where I told him I didn't understand him not grasping the basics of the project and that he was not performing. I concluded by telling him to get the project completed!

When we attended the next update meeting, the business analyst stated he was having trouble with the data coming in from the source. Just an aside, this data had been coming in from that source for years in the same format without a problem. Also, the analyst started floating the idea that we should abandon this selected tool and engage the bank for a "more accurate solution." We looked at that change and saw it would delay the proof of concept by another twelve to sixteen weeks at the minimum.

At this point, the project was getting out of control. Therefore, we chose not to go the riskier more accurate solution and proceeded with the original project. The proof of concept was finally finished, and the demonstration worked, our assignment was completed. But I gave the analyst poor marks for his performance and didn't use him again.

The lessons learned in this small project is they can have the same issues as big ones. Especially where the analyst didn't listen to the details of the assignment. He wanted to change the solution to the "ultimate" one without delivering what has been initially agreed upon with our internal client.

March of 2020 was another sad time in my life. I lost my ninety-two-year-old Mom due to heart failure and no it wasn't due to COVID-19 even though she was in an assisted living facility. Mom started having heart problems when she was forty-nine with a heart attack. The problems continued over the years but she lasted forty-three years after that first heart attack. Her death was expected when the need for heart valve surgery was discouraged because she wouldn't survive the three separate surgeries needed to fix the problem and at that point, she was given three months to live. Even though it was expected it was a terrible loss, she was my rock, and I miss her every day!

In May of 2020, the Productivity Enhancement CFO Sponsor left the company, COVID-19 was growing, and the company finished reorganizing and furloughed several employees. Internal company political intrigue was high with everyone, and everything being looked at under a microscope. When these conditions exist in a company, projects get stalled because previous strategies and plans are reviewed and second guessed. In my case the company decided to cut out several consultants and redistribute the workload internally. I was cut, it would have been nice to have seen the projects through to completion, but being cut is a normal thing in consulting business and has happened before during my career.

IV

CREATING BEAUTY

CHAPTER 17

CONSCIOUSNESS

I view the events at my client and COVID-19 as the perfect time to transition for the third time. Even with my two previous transitions, I keep feeling that I missed something along the way—a home base, a refuge, place to recharge and relax. I started by considering the questions I needed to answer in finding the missing link. Maybe I will find the thing I hadn't found by having many homes around the world. Maybe I'm a citizen of the world because I'm comfortable anywhere in the world. Maybe I don't need a single place to be my home base. Maybe **I'm** home base and the things I do every day doesn't need a location—enjoying each experience as they come and remembering not to rush just to move on to the next thing.

I was living in my condominium in the Buckhead part of Atlanta, but I had become more unhappy with living there. The Atlanta Mayor had instituted a policy of not prosecute minor crimes. That policy led to an increase in more severe crimes, increasing Police response times, and lowering their morale. Things came to a head for me when we had riots in May 2020 in my neighborhood and outside my building. Looting, destroying property, and automatic gunfire. A friend, in another condominium, had a bullet go through his floor to ceiling glass window and lodge in his inner wall. The city that I loved had changed and I knew it would take years for it to come back. I decided to sell my condominium and as luck would have it, I sold it in two days at a good price. My preference was to move back to the suburbs in an area I had previously lived. I looked for a house to buy for several months, while staying with Jennifer, but the prices were too high and going even higher, so I decided to rent an apartment and look for a house at a time when prices were more reasonable.

With my decision on location being made, my next step in my reinvention was to rely on my previous reinvention process. Starting with self-reflection. This self-reflection had to be done with complete honesty while evaluating events and how I had handled them. I also evaluated my progress on personal and professional development. I reviewed my core values and assessed my strengths, skills, accomplishment, and failures. I also include those work and life things that were undesirable and shouldn't be repeated.

I noted many areas of myself and life where I need improvement. Such as:

- I'm constantly moving on to something else, a bit of a nomad.
- I'm a bystander, an observer, and it takes time for me to engage.
- I'm constantly searching.

As before, my notes were extensive and once I had the good, bad, and ugly laid out, I could clearly see what the reinvention looked like. I again sought input and advice from others to adjust my future vision and purpose.

My mission in the past was driven by companies, peers, and family. Not saying that was wrong but I felt the need to evolve. In this reinvention my mission is to contribute by sharing impactful stories through photography and words with the goal of expanding consciousness through people's understanding of the world. There is a lack of definition of consciousness even after millions of analyses, debates, and research. To me it's the awareness of internal and external existence. It's a set of shared beliefs and ideas, excluding politics, which operate to form a society that shares knowledge and promotes creativity.

<u>My focus:</u>

- "Transition to a higher level of consciousness through a deeper exploration into my creativity."
- "Make a contribution to the world by sharing life stories, creativity, knowledge, and beautiful photographic images."

I will deliver my mission by creating impactful photos, written works, and sharing lessons learned through coaching while keeping my focus on family and friends.

My creative process, which has developed over time, is to come up with an idea and then to use both science and art to add the detail. For the science part I do research, analyze information and create a plan. The art part is where I add the emotion, feeling and the message I want to convey. If you've read Arthur Koestler's "The Act of Creation" you will notice at a high level the similarities. The creative process is a good base to launch into the world of Photography and Writing. Breaking into these two new industries requires more than being creative. There is also the technical, business, and industry cultural aspects.

I chose to follow my previous process by diving into the details of these three industries. Step one is to study the industry by reading books, following top experts, take some courses, make connections in the industry, join networking associations, and staying up to date on industry news. The next step is to define who I am in that industry. In photography should I be in Fine Arts, Commercial, Photojournalism, Wedding, or Portrait Photography? In writing do I focus on fiction or non-fiction writing? Do I write novels, articles, blogs, or commercial content? In coaching, in what area do I focus given the long list of recognized disciplines. The third step is to define the details in a chosen area, my focus definition. In addition, learning all aspects of the technical side of each industry such as equipment, software, and techniques. While this accelerated industry learning process is going on the steps to start a business must also be addressed, such as finances, marketing, sales, product production and delivery.

All these tasks seemed overwhelming unless I apply my approach of breaking them down into smaller, bite size, pieces which I've done with many clients on complex projects. My mind set is that my road ahead was navigable, but it would take time and setting interim doable goals is critical.

Photography

I've always admired the many great storytelling photographers such as Robert Capa, Henri Cartier-Bresson, Annie Leibovitz, Ralph Gibson, and James Nachtwey.

"I feel it is the heart, not the eye, that should determine the content of the photograph." – Gordon Parks, photographer

"To photograph truthfully and effectively is to see beneath the surfaces." – Ansel Adams, photographer

Storytelling through photography confronts the reality that must be captured and shared with feeling. My passion is taking photographs, and my primary interest lies in the photographic genres of landscape, cityscape, and abstract, each with the vast array of stories to tell.

When I shoot a photography, I want to capture images that are impactful, sparking feelings, and imagination. If I <u>can't</u>, the photos won't tell the story I want to tell and won't speak to the viewer. I must look behind the photography, a lesson that became crystal clear on my 2005 photo shoot in Paris.

Photographs can impact the world by taking people to places and circumstances they haven't been before and expanding their level of consciousness, this is my photographic vision.

I began to recognize the fun of photography in the early 1950s. My family used a Kodak Duaflex II, taking pictures of our family and friends. Dad loved cameras and was a good photographer, but Mom seemed to find a way to have a finger cover part of the lens in every shot she took, which ruined the shot. That recognition became fascination in 1959 when we were in Ft. Rucker, AL and I got a Kodak Brownie Starlet camera for Christmas. The camera used 127 roll black and white film which I immediately loaded into the camera and started taking photos. My first shots were of odd things such as the inside of garbage cans. One of those photos I liked the most was the inside of a galvanized trash can that contained one small empty coke bottle. When the film was developed, I felt great pride looking at my masterpiece and showed my family, my father's reaction was to shake his head in disbelief. He loved to take pictures and didn't understand the waste of film on such odd things.

My photography was sporadic with periods of no photos at all until 1963, while living in Paris, I purchased a Minolta SR7 and started shooting 35mm color slides. I loved the slide format and took the camera with me everywhere. By the time we left Paris, I had accumulated thousands of slides. Unfortunately, during our trip back to the U.S. the movers lost most of the boxes of slides. It was by chance that about one hundred slides survived because they were packed separately. I still have the memory of those lost photos tucked away in my mind's slide tray.

Coming back to the U.S., attending college and starting my business career left little time for photography. My photography was limited to taking photos of family, friends, and vacation. I did upgrade to the Minolta XD11 in 1977 and continued this same genre.

It wasn't until September of 1999, when I purchased a Nikon N70 that I started to take photography more seriously. I was traveling 75% of the time for work and taking the N70 wasn't practical so I picked up a small Fuji film FinePix A303 to take on the road. In 2004 I moved to digital photography and bought a Nikon D70 and then in 2013 a Nikon D800. Since I continued to travel for work, I bought a CoolPix S9900 in 2015 for those trips. Over the years I've tried several cameras searching for the perfect one. It was after studying many of the famous photographers that I realized it wasn't the equipment, it was the photographer that made the good shots. I now advise beginners to start with one camera and one lens and not to immediately search for the perfect equipment. Shoot with the one camera and lens for at least a year, getting to know each well. Doing that will help to learn the basics of photography such as lighting, focus, composition, and most importantly the photographer's eye.

I'm currently using a Nikon Z6 II and my go to lens is a Z 24-70mm. Most of my learning now is the post processing with the ever-changing tools such as Photoshop, Lightroom, and add-ons such as Topaz. The latest trends of digital image creation and Artificial Intelligence also require my understanding because they're wildly expanding the art of photography.

Before I started this latest transformation there were key decisions to make in creating a photography plan for success. I needed to decide what genre of photographs to shoot and defining my unique style of photos. The subject of my photos evolved and when I made my move to digital cameras, I was shooting anything that looked like a good shot. The freedom of the digital format meant I could shoot more without the expense of developing them to see what I had. However, I know that to become the best required me to narrow my subjects to what interest me the most. I chose to concentrate on Landscape, Cityscape, and Abstract. That's not to say if I see an interesting subject I won't take it.

The definitions of the three genres I chose are: Landscape - *Landscape photography is capturing the beauty of scenic views.* Cityscape - *Cityscape photography is an artistic representation of the physical and people aspects of a city or urban area.* Abstract - *The use of perspective, movement, and light to transform the world we see into an unexpected, often unrecognizable image.* I understand that narrowing my list of preferred genres from hundreds of genres, sub-genres, and sub-sub-genres to three seems like an accomplishment but the depth of effort, knowledge, and practice to succeed in each one is vast. I continue to hone my skills and knowledge in each area which may lead to a further narrowing of my genre selection.

I continue to work on the tools and techniques of photography with the goal to never stop learning and adapting to the industry changes.

Writing

As with photographers, authors tell stories but with a deferent media. Some of the notables are Homer, Charles Dickens, William Shakespeare, Mark Twain, and Stephen King.

The very reason I write is so that I might not sleepwalk through my entire life." - Zadie Smith, author

"The truth is we write for love." – Erica Jong, author

The clinical reasons writers write have been summed up with the phrases to describe, to entertain, to explain or inform, or to persuade. However, if you ask writers why they write their reasons are much more personal. Some write because they feel they were born to write and feel empty when they aren't writing. Others have something to say, and writing gets it out. It's also said that writing creates conversations that span time and space.

"Nothing ever seems to me quite real at the moment it happens. That's all one tries to do in writing, really, to hold something—the past, the present." - Gore Vidal, author

Writing is an art, like photography, and as an artist I'm passionate about my creations and desire to tell a story. If I do it right, it will be impactful.

My approach to penetrating this industry was the same as photography with some critical differences. Unlike photography my writing experience is non-existent and possibly hurt by the business writing of reports, speeches, and emails.

I was lucky to connect with Rosemary Daniell, an excellent author, coach, and mentor. Rosemary helped me to define my first work which was, write a book to share my business lessons learned because of my decades of business experience. I spent several months working on the book until one session with Rosemary when we looked at each other and simultaneously said "This book is dull." That meeting helped me to change direction and write this book, "Bring Your Best Game," my memoir using selective stories, and still sharing business lessons and adding life lessons.

After completing the book my education and attention turn to the next phase of this project, which included agents, publishing, marketing, sales, and distribution. This part of the process is more complex, difficult, and lengthy than writing the book. I can say the entire experience of writing this book and getting it published has been personally rewarding. I haven't only learned more about the industry and became reacquainted with my life experiences.

My goal is to combine photography and writing into stories that take my audience to the core of the human experience and emotions.

<u>Coaching</u>

I read an article that listed and described thirty-one types of coaching and there are probably other lists that are longer. The point is that coaching is such a large area with various labels it can get quite confusing and fail to offer concrete direction when choosing a coach. The training and certification for these coaching areas vary as well. The one consistent guideline put forth is a Code of Ethics, an essential component for the credibility of the coaching world.

My coaching experience goes back to the beginning of my business career where I worked with individual employees and managers under various circumstances. Later, during my consulting career I was considered a trusted advisor to several executives. Now that I'm pursuing this area in my third reinvention, I wanted to define my offerings to better engage clients. Reviewing the list of types I concluded I could fall into six of the categories:

- Life and Career—redefinition, achieving balance, and setting goals.
- Business—Focusing on executives, improving performance and growth.
- Transformation—reinvention.
- Performance—removing roadblocks, boosting effectiveness, and productivity.
- Success—how to get from NOW to FUTURE.
- Strategy—mapping the plan forward and incorporating change.

There is a wide range of circumstances that would prompt a need for a coach. It could be from wanting to bring fresh perspective into the current situation, to having a need to correct pressing problems, to a reinvention that completely changes their course.

The circumstances may be different, but the successful methods of coaching I've used are consistent. My objective is to help people and businesses to assess their current situation, define a path to the future, develop a plan to achieve that future, and coaching to success.

The first step in the approach to ramping up this area of reinvention is to update my methodology, tools, and techniques previously used. I also need to update my marketing collaterals and social media. Next assessing my shortfall in skills, education, and certifications needed and filling those gaps. The final step is network, network, and network.

The three areas of photography, writing and coaching define my Third Reinvention. My goals are to continue to write, to promote my photography and become a recognized professional photographer whose work is prized, launch my coaching practice, and to enjoy life each day.

V

EPILOGUE

BRINGING GAME

It has been said that we must be passionate about what we do to be successful. I agree that passion is a big piece, so is knowledge, concentration, practice, and commitment. Having heart, never quitting, bringing your "A" game, all enhance success. Even people who are working each day in something they don't like needs to bring their "A" game to achieve individual success which reinforces a positive attitude. Success can be what you're doing now, and along with a positive attitude will lead to doing what you love.

Success is a topic that has been discussed, written about, in movies and documentaries, and probably carved on ancient walls. I believe success is summed up by knowledge, experience, performance, professionalism, and results.

More specifically:
- Study the industry, company, and job you're in to determine the skills and behavior required.

- Seek advice and form relationships with experienced people.

- Read books, articles, trade publications and listen to Podcasts and other media.

- Make connections and network by attending events, conferences, and shows.

- Understand the performance requirements to be successful and deliver the results.

- Adapt to your environment.

- Always conduct yourself as a professional.

- Don't compromise on your ethics.

- Accepting there are no short cuts. Do the work.

- Step outside your comfort zone and tackle new things.

- Don't quit!

This success approach, as it evolved throughout my life, has served me well while pursuing sharpshooting, international business, and now art. For example, my adaptation skills started to form when I was five sleeping on a military cot in a two-room dwelling in Missouri and evolved with each new country, city, home, job, and challenge over the years. A key to adapting is accepting change and figuring out how to make the best, and even learn, from it. Given the adapt and change skill developed, I've sought out reinvention to expand knowledge and move closer to my life's passion.

I've learned many things working, living, and traveling around the world. A couple of observations standout, such as the principles of life doesn't change. Fads or the *next big thing* rarely produce the results advertised and aren't lasting. I remember one evening over dinner discussing the dot-com craze, which was going on at the time, with a business partner in Ireland. He forcefully stated, "This doesn't make sense, it goes against all tested business practices. It can't last." He was correct it was a bubble that burst. A few people did make money, but many people didn't. While I embrace change and innovation, I struggle to justify the risks while my heart pulls me to be an early adopter.

Another observation is that people around the world want the same things. They want to work, to take care of their families, have pride in what they do, and be a part of something meaningful. What they don't want, as many have told me with animated emotion, is their governments on their backs.

I charge into my third reinvention as an artist and taking along the volumes of lessons learned. My commitment is to do what I love and bring my "Best Game" every day, I will continue to transition and reinvent along the way and loving the journey as I go. Who knows, there may be a fourth reinvention coming.

The world is vast, full of excitement, and wondrous beauty with millions of stories to tell. I look forward to recording and sharing more stories and lessons.

UNTIL NEXT TIME

VI

NOTEWORTHY LESSONS

Phrases, quotes, soundbites have an impact on us. The challenge is to short out what is useful and what is just B.S. and keep the productive ones. Below are some of the ones I've kept and that have helped me through my journey:

<u>Passion</u>

- With a passion one gives their all to the point of exhaustion.
- You must find your passion.
- Your passion is your purpose.
- It was meant to be.
- I collect art because the works nourishes the soul and excites the mind. My life is better because these artists create such beautiful pieces.
- There is something outside me that must be served.

<u>Future</u>

- You must have something to look forward to.
- Everyone needs a goal, something to work for.
- You either have a reason or don't.
- Every journey is full of wonder.
- You are always trying to get back home.

• Men in the autumn of their life fear not being relevant, important, a player. They don't understand that everyone can be productive and creative until the last breath. Van Gogh only lived for 37 years and made an impact on the world. Clint Eastwood is still creating at 90. It's not how long you live, it's what you do with those years.

Reinvention

• You must reinvent yourself several times in your life.

• Will he ever walk away? Will he ever walk again? Yes, if he decides he has someplace to go.

Performance

• It's the mental game.

• It's the successes that are earned by work, fight, sweat, and blood that are the most rewarding. Successes bestowed but unearned are hollow.

• Focus, focus, focus.

• Deliver more than you promise.

• Don't get overwhelmed by the size of the work.

• Every large task is done one piece at a time.

• Your metal is tested when all hell breaks loose.

• Simplicity is order.

• Innovate; create things that serve the individual needs.

• On your birthday you should finish or do one last challenge of the year.

• If you sleep even a day, you get passed up.

• Never, ever, give up

<u>Leadership</u>

- Leaders are given authority by their team.

- There is a big difference in being a tough-minded manager than a SOB. Tough means saying, "You messed up and you can't do it again. Now Let's see how you can prevent it from occurring again. Let's learn." A SOB criticizes, berates, yells and does not help you learn and improve.

- Everyone is far more capable than companies or managers give them credit.

- Context over dogma?

- Help one person at a time.

VII

SOURCES

1. A Child Goes to Europe

- TWA Constellation (Super Connie), In *Wikipedia.*
  - *wikipedia.org/wiki/Lockheed_Constellation*
- Simca, In *Wikipedia.*
  - *wikipedia.org/wiki/Simca*
- Battle of Metz. (2021, May 13). In *WW2-history. Fandom.*
  - *ww2-history.fandom.com/wiki/Battle_of_Metz*
- Saarbrücken. (2021, May 13). In *Britannica.*
  - *britannica.com/place/Saarbrucken*

2. Happiness & Horror

- McGraw Kaserne, Munich, Germany, In *Wikipedia.*
  - *wikipedia.org/wiki/McGraw_Kaserne*
- Rudolph, O. (Director). (1955). *False Accusations* [Film]. General Service Studios.
- Copelan, J. (Director). (1956). *The Plastic Ghost* [Film]. McGowan Productions.
- Blair, G. (Director). (1956). *Horse Crazy* [Film]. Roy Rogers Productions.
- Dachau. (2020, October 1). In *Britannica.*
  - *britannica.com/place/Dachau-concentration-camp-Germany*
- 1956 Hungarian Revolution. (2022, March 7). In *History Channel.*
  - *history.com/this-day-in-history/soviets-put-brutal-end-to-hungarian-revolution*

- 1956 Poznan Protests. (2020, October 1). In *polishhistory.pl.*
  - *polishhistory.pl/poznan-1956-a-revolt-that-shook-the-system*

3. Coming Home

- Fort Rucker, Alabama. armybases.org.
  - *armybases.org/fort-rucker-al-alabama*
- UNIVAC, In *Wikipedia.*
  - *wikipedia.org/wiki/UNIVAC*
- 1959 Kitchen Debate. (2021, August 30). In *Association for Diplomatic Studies & Training.*
  - *adst.org/2015/07/nixon-vs-khrushchev-the-1959-kitchen-debate*
- 1961 Bay of Pigs. (2022, August 30). In *CIA Stories.*
  - *cia.gov/stories/story/the-bay-of-pigs-invasion*
- Nader, R. (1965). *Unsafe at Any Speed.* Grossman Publishers

4. A Young Man Goes to Paris

- International Baccalaureate program, In *IBO website.*
  - *ibo.org/about-the-ib*
- Barbizon School of Painters, Barbizon, France, In *Wikipedia.*
  - *wikipedia.org/wiki/Barbizon_School*
- Rodin Museum. (2021, October 1). In *Musee Rodin.*
  - *musee-rodin.fr*

5. University, Draft & Marriage

- Dominican Republic Civil War, In *Oxford Bibliographies.*
  - *oxfordbibliographies.com/display/document/obo-9780199766581/obo-9780199766581-0071*
- Paris, France Population in 1965, In *Macrotrends.net.*
  - *macrotrends.net/cities/20985/paris/population*
- Five Stages of Grief, In *Cleveland Clinic.org.*
  - *health.clevelandclinic.org/5-stages-of-grief*
- 1969 Moon Landing, In *NASA.gov.*

- - o *nasa.gov/history/july-20-1969-one-giant-leap-for-mankind*
- Kent State Shootings, In *Wikipedia.*
  - o *wikipedia.org/wiki/Kent_State_shootings*

6. Great Mentors

- Ruta Lee, In *rutalee.com.*
  - o *rutalee.com/biography.html*
- John W. Teets, In johnwteets.com.
  - o *johnwteets.com/Bio*

8. Time for a Change

- J Paul Austin, In *Wikipedia.*
  - o *wikipedia.org/wiki/J._Paul_Austin*

9. New Career

- Bosworth, M. (1995). *Solution Selling.* McGraw Hill.
- Holden, J. (1990). *Power Base Selling.* John Wiley & Sons, Inc.

10. The Big Ones

- Neville Chamberlain. (2020, October 1). In *National Archives UK.*
  - o *nationalarchives.gov.uk/education/resources/chamberlain-and-hitler*

11. Struggling to Transition

- Spencer, L. (2008). *Touching History.* Free Press.
- Robert Wise (Director), (1951), *The Day the World Stood Still,* 20th Century Fox.

12. Finding a Niche

- Ansel Adams. In *Ansel Adams website.*
  - o *anseladams.com*
- Ralph Gibson. In *Ralph Gibson website.*

- o *ralphgibson.com*
- Elliott Erwitt. In *Elliott Erwitt website.*
- o *elliotterwitt.com*

13. Quick Successes & Terrible Loss

- NASSCOM. In *NASSCOM website.*
- o *nasscom.in*
- Ciprofloxacin. In *Mayo Clinic website.*
- o *mayoclinic.org/drugs-supplements/ciprofloxacin-oral-route/description/drg-20072288*

14. Attempting Consistency

- Rosemary Daniell, Zona Rosa. In *MyZonaRosa website.*
- o *therosemarydaniell.com*

15. Turmoil, Adventure & Sadness

- Tiananmen Square. (2020, October 1). In *BBC, Amnesty UK.*
- o *bbc.com/news/world-asia-48445934*
- o *amnesty.org.uk/china-1989-tiananmen-square-protests-demonstration-massacre*
- Forbidden City. (2020, October 1). In *China Highlights.*
- o *chinahighlights.com/beijing/forbidden-city/#:~:text=The Forbidden City took 14,10 of the Qing Dynasty*
- JuYongGuan Great Wall. (2020, October 1). In *China Tour Guide.*
- o *chinatourguide.com/Great_Wall/Juyong_Pass_Great_Wall*
- Temple of Heaven. (2021, October 26). In *China Highlights.*
- o *chinahighlights.com/beijing/attraction/temple-of-heaven*
- Summer Palace. (2021, October 26). In *China Highlights.*
- o *chinahighlights.com/beijing/attraction/summer-palace*
- Old Summer Palace. (2021, October 26). In *China Highlights.*
- o *chinahighlights.com/beijing/attraction/old-summer-palace*
- 60 Minutes Australia. (2019, February 21). *Inside China's ghost cities.*

- o *youtube.com/watch?v=Ie6zd3Rwu4c*
- 1842 Treaty of Nanking. (1901, December 13). In *USC US-China Institute.*
  - o *china.usc.edu/treaty-nanjing-nanking-1842*

16. Needle's Eye

- No Sources for this chapter.

17. Transitioning to a Hight Level

- Koestler, A. (2023). *The Act of Creation.* Penguin Press.
- Sandra Roussy. In *Sandra Roussy website and Digital Photography School.*
  - o *sandraroussy.com*
  - o *digital-photography-school.com/author/sandra-roussy*

EPILOGUE - BRING YOUR BEST GAME

- No Sources for the EPILOGUE.

USEFUL PHRASES - BRING YOUR BEST GAME

- No Sources for the USEFUL PHRASES.